The Universe and Its Creation

The probability of God and Improbability of Science

Order this book online at www.trafford.com
or email orders@trafford.com

Most Trafford titles are also available at major online book retailers.

The author argues that the Big Bang theory offers no certainty in the creation of
the universe, and challenges the views that it offers justice to understand reality.
The Big Bang theory is just a quest for denying the existence of God.

Printed in the United States of America.

ISBN: 978-1-4269-6278-3 (sc)

Trafford rev. 03/18/2011

 www.trafford.com

North America & international
toll-free: 1 888 232 4444 (USA & Canada)
phone: 250 383 6864 ♦ fax: 812 355 4082

Contents

"Many scientists do believe in both science and God, the God of revelation, in a perfectly consistent way." — Richard Feynman, Nobel laureate in physics

Preface

Little has been revealed concerning the formation of the universe. Prevailing theories state that the atom was composed of subatomic matters that exploded outward, multiplied, and diversified to form the omniuniverse. The atom itself is known to be the great seed of the universe.

Science suggests that the universe expands steadily, and its density reduces to the present density which is now less than 10^{-30} grams per cubic centimeter. Thus, if we traveled back in time, we would live in a universe with a higher density. Ultimately, we would arrive at the very high density state, popularly called the "Big Bang" (other expressions were in use such as singular state or big squeeze), where the density could be more than 10^{10} grams per cubic centimeter.

Cosmologists, however, still debate the reality of the Big Bang theory. Eddington and other scientists were against the idea of the Big Bang that begins in a dense state. The idea of steady state expansion of the universe attracted many cosmologists who disliked the Big Bang idea, and many believe that the Big Bang theory was mistaken, and they also believe that the idea was more sensational than sensible. George Lemaitre developed and championed a dense origin that he referred to as the "primeval atom". He suggested that the universe resembles the primeval atom of a huge radioactivity, which exploded and formed fragments that evolved into galaxies and stars. Lemaitre was a priest and some cosmologists viewed his theory as an amalgam of theology and science.

Cosmologists suggested that the formation of the universe passed through three stages; the lepton era, the radiation era and the matter era. The lepton era was the highest density where muons, neutrinos, and electrons (we will discuss them in later) were the origin of the universe. The lepton era then passed to the radiation era where alpha, beta, and gamma rays were dominant. In the radiation era large quantities of helium were produced due to the alpha radiation. Protons and neutrons were exchanged to produce the matter through interactions of their subatomic particles called quarks and leptons. Energy was also produced due to the interaction of the subatomic particles. The matter gained mass through the interaction with the so called "Higgs field" that is not yet observed physically.

The Large Hadrons Collider (LHC) between France and Switzerland has been built to investigate the reality of the formation of the universe through the annihilation of protons and electrons to observe Higgs boson, black holes, weak energy, and other subatomic interactions.

This book illustrates wide ranges of these interactions, from planetary atoms to dark matter, from proton-proton interaction to the CNO (carbon, nitrogen, and oxygen) cycle, and from the annihilation of quarks and leptons to released energy.

This book is a real journey into many modern physics including quantum physics and the chemistry of the evolution of the universe. Undergraduates, graduates, and postgraduates will enjoy this book. The book describes a revolution in particle physics in our understanding the mystery and beauty of the universe.

Mathematically, the book shows that science can not prove the imbalanced force and momentum between the sun and its orbiting planets. The analysis also demonstrates that the earth and the solar planets are not conjoined to the sun in their orbit. Therefore, the analysis in this book reinforces theology over science.

Because it has some valid scientific points, the Big Bang theory is an interesting and valuable scientific theory, and it is one of the best theories that materialists have been using to justify that God has nothing to do with the creation of the universe. However, it is demonstrably inadequate, to say the least. The Big Bang theory cannot explain the origin of the universe just by saying the universe was created from nothingness. Scientists can not absorb that galaxies and our planet were made from nothing.

This book shows the scientific and philosophical weaknesses of the Big Bang theory by pointing out the contradiction of many cores of the theory. Written on a level that scientifically uneducated people can comprehend, it fairly proves the intellectual superiority of God in the creation of the universe as given in the holy books.

With the amazing attractiveness of recent books supporting agnosticism or atheism, the objective of the materialists is to pervade hedonistic and debauched procedures uncovered under the umbrella of the idea that "the universe was created spontaneously and no involvement of God."

The author tackles a wealth of evidence when he scientifically talks about the temperature of the expansion of the universe, the red shift, the Higgs field, space time relativity, the wormholes effect, and the quantum vacuum of the electromagnetic field

The author argues that the Big Bang theory offers no certainty in the creation of the universe, and challenges the views that it offers justice to understand reality. The Big Bang theory is just a quest for denying the existence of God.

By: Amin Elsersawi, Ph.D.

Introduction

The medieval astronomers and cosmologists who wrote in Greek, Arabic, Latin, and Hebrew were all heavily influenced by Ptolemy's theories of cosmology. Ptolemy's cosmology was held in high regard by cosmologists in Greece, Rome, Arabia, and Egypt.

In 1943, Nicolas Copernicus (1473-1543) wrote a book which set forth his idea of a heliocentric planetary system. Only about 5% of the book was actually composed of his revolutionary theory. The rest of the book was just a rewrite of Ptolemy's theories. Copernicus hypothesis was that the sun was located at the centre of the universe. This contradicted the theory of Ptolemy, in which the earth was at the centre of the universe.

Galileo Galilei (1564 –1642) an Italian physicist, was named the "father of modern observational astronomy". His achievements include improvements to the telescope and consequent astronomical observations, and support for Copernicanism.

Edwin Hubble (1889-1953) was a pioneering American astronomer responsible for several extremely important scientific advances in the early and mid 20th century. By the time of his death in 1953, he was widely regarded as one of the greatest astronomers ever. The Hubble Space Telescope, the most productive space-based telescope in history, is named after him. Hubble's Law, which declares that the further away a galaxy is, the greater a redshift it will have.

Recently, little has been revealed concerning the formation of the universe. Prevailing theories state that the atom was composed of subatomic matter that exploded outward, multiplied, and diversified to form the omniuniverse through the so called Higgs field which gives mass to every elementary particle. Scientifically, the atom itself is assumed to be the great seed of the universe.

It is well known that the universe expands steadily. Its density reduces to the present density, which is now less than 10^{-30} grams per cubic centimeter. Thus, if we traveled back in time, we would live in a universe with a much higher density. Ultimately, we would arrive at the very highly dense state, universally called the "Big Bang" (other expressions used are "singular state" or "big squeeze"), where the density could be more than 10^{10} grams per cubic centimeter. The Hindu religion (6000 years ago) believes in nothingness (singularity) as the start point of the Big Bang.

Cosmologists, however, still debate the reality of the Big Bang theory. Arthur Stanley Eddington (1882 –1944) was a British astrophysicist of the early 20th century, and was unconvinced by the Big Bang theory. The idea of a steady state of the expansion of the universe attracted many cosmologists who disliked the Big Bang idea. Many believe that the Big Bang theory was mistaken, and they also believe that the idea was more exciting than it really is. George Lemaitre developed and championed a dense origin that he referred to as the "primeval atom". He suggested that the universe resembles the primeval atom of a huge radioactivity, which exploded and formed fragments that evolved into galaxies and stars. Lemaitre was a priest and some cosmologists viewed his theory as an amalgam of theology and science.

When Charles Darwin, in the middle of the nineteenth century, launched his Evolution theory, a conflict between religions' pieties and science started. Darwin and Galileo agitated the followers of Plato (idealist philosopher) and Bishop George Berkeley (in more recent time), until the Christians Association of Stellar Explorers (CASE) was established to mend the rift with science and religion.

Religion, for example, says that the creation of the entire universe occurred on day one, within this literal six days of controlling and adapting the creation of humans, animals, trees, etc. The rift with science increased when scientists assumed several theories (such as the Big Bang theory, the Quantum theory by Einstein, and the latest Eleven - Dimension Universe by Arkani-Hamid) to explain the formation of the universe.

The universe seems designed specifically for life. Physical constants such as the strength of gravity, the mass of the proton, and the charge of electrons appear so finely tuned that the smallest variation would prohibit life in the cosmos. This design implies intelligence, and such intelligence implies a fundamental attribute of God, or infinite Mind, and purpose to humanity's existence. From the complexity of the global environment to quantum physics, and relativity through the work of Neils Bohr, Paul Dirac and John Von Neuman, religion conceived God as the supernatural creator, overseer of the universe, and the designer and sustainer of the vast universe.

Gravity, mass, protons with quarks, leptons and weak and strong energy don't feel compassion, ethics, honour or empathy. These emotions are all evidence that can be supportive of the divine. It is impossible for a physical system, no matter how complex it is, to process sense, to process creativity, or to process sentiment.

It is therefore necessary to discuss the importance of ethical transformations to a life of love and character, as the development of a technological society does not free us from ethical demands.

As science developed from the 19th century onwards, various views developed which aimed to reconcile science with the Genesis creation narrative. The Institute on Religion in an Age of Science (IRAS) is an independent society of scientists, philosophers, religious scholars, theologians, and others who want to understand the role of religion in our dynamic scientific world. Each year, IRAS holds a week-long conference on Star Island off the coast of Portsmouth, New Hampshire and organizes events at the annual meetings of the American Association for the Advancement of Science and the American Academy of Religion. The organizers envision the establishment of several tax-exempt foundations to further these bold efforts.

With the historian it is an article of faith that knowledge of the past is a key to understanding the present. Across the academic communities of the world, there is a new openness to the interaction of God with the development of world history, and growing numbers of people are allowing for a meta-physical explanation of the physical nature of the universe. Scientists often acknowledge a sense of the divine from looking at life on earth and at order in the universe. For example, the efficiency of DNA as a carrier of data is so great that if all the information held in all the libraries of the world were programmed onto DNA, that information would fit on about one percent of the head of a pin. Yet the human brain has ten thousand times the capacity for information than the human genome does (Schroeder 1997). This seems all the more significant when one considers that the human brain has the capacity to store the information contained in a 50 million volume encyclopedia.

Six years ago, the Princeton Theological Seminary established a chair dedicated to science and theology. The products of the Princeton's Centre for Theological Inquiry and the Princeton Theological Seminary together represent a major thrust in the study of the religious-scientific union. Their efforts promise to be novel and historic. In 1995, Davies won the Templeton Prize for Progress in Religion after the publication of his book The Mind of God: The Scientific Basis for a Rational World. Sir John Templeton's financial contributions to the National Institute for Healthcare Research are also noted. The Institute is promoting research on religion, devoting its time to "spiritual progress" quantifying that religion is beneficial to one's health.

The author concluded by making it quite clear that he holds to a "God created the universe" view. He also clarified common misunderstandings about what recent cosmological scientists say so that the reader can intelligently understands these uncertain ideas.

This book illustrates wide ranges of these interactions, from planetary atoms to dark matter, from proton-proton interaction to the CNO (carbon, nitrogen, and oxygen) cycle, and from the annihilation of quarks and leptons to the energy released.

This book is a real journey into many modern physics including quantum physics and the chemistry of the evolution of the universe. Undergraduates, graduates, and postgraduates will enjoy this book. The book describes a revolution in particle physics in our understanding the mystery and beauty of the universe.

The book is written for the well-read layman from the high school to the university level, explored and explained the historical development of the universe, including current ideas in the field.

The author also briefly explained, among other things, quantum mechanics, general relativity, the string theory, the cosmological constant, the Hubble constant, dark matter, dark energy and fundamental particles of the atom. For modern cosmology, he discussed the Big Bang in detail and, more briefly, the Steady-State model and the Plasma Universe model.

Mathematically, the book shows that science cannot prove the imbalanced force and momentum between the sun and its orbiting planets. The analysis also demonstrates that the earth and the solar planets are not conjoined to the sun in their spinning. Therefore, the analysis in this book reinforces theology over science.

1. Keywords

Solar System, Milky Way, precession of the Earth' axis, Big Bang and Big Crunch, Hubble's Principle, mass of planets, sun, and galaxy, weak nuclear force, theory of de Sitter-like Universe, galaxy rotation curve, God does not play dice in the universe by Einstein, quantum cosmology, theories of the formation of the universe, quarks and leptons stage, alpha decay, beta decay, gamma rays, building blocks of matter, fermions and bosons, standard model, matters and antimatters, decay of protons, neutrons and fermions, Feynman diagram, grand unified theory, the Higgs boson and field, proton and antiproton collision, supersymmetry, string theory, the Large Hadron Collider (LHC), sun corona, heliosphere, solar wind, nuclear atmosphere, p-p chains, CNO cycle, the Oh-My-God Particles, Jewish, Christian, and Muslim traditions, quotations, Euler Method, Angular Momentum, Gravitational Attraction

2. Abstracts

Galileo Galilee was punished for his suggestion that the Earth revolves around the Sun, a scientific theory that threatened the Church's place in the world. In that time, the Roman Catholics believed that Purgatory was in a place in the universe where souls remain until they have expiated their sins and then they can go to heaven.

When Charles Darwin, in the middle of the nineteenth century, launched his Evolution theory, a conflict between religions' pieties and science started. Darwin and Galileo agitated the followers of Plato (idealist philosopher) and Bishop George Berkeley (in more recent time), until the Christians Association of Stellar Explorers (CASE) was established to mend the rift with science and religion.
Religion, for example, says that the creation of the entire universe occurred on day one, within this literal six days of controlling and adapting the creation of humans, animals, trees, etc. The rift with science increased when scientists assumed several theories (such as the Big Bang theory, the Quantum theory by Einstein, and the latest Eleven - Dimension Universe by Arkani-Hamid) to explain the formation of the universe.
This book discusses the beliefs of the three religions, Jewish, Christian, and Muslim, and their traditions in understanding the universe, and science.

In this analysis, we correlate our planet to the Sun, and the Sun to the galaxy (Milky Way), and the Galaxy to the Universe, considering the mass and velocity position of each individual planet in their revolutions. Euler method is being used in this investigation.

Also, angular Momentum and Gravitational Attraction were calculated to show that the planets and the Sun are not associated to each other, as the science proclaimed.

Mathematically, all results showed bias in favour of religions.

3. Early Theories of Cosmology

Ptolemy created a universe that lasted a thousand years. Copernicus created a universe that lasted four hundred years. Einstein has created a universe, and I can't tell you how long it will last. George Bernard Shaw

Ptolemy (or Claudius Ptolemaeus or Klaudios Ptolemaios)) lived in Alexandria, Egypt, from approx. 87 to probably 170 AD. Very little is known about his personal life. He was speculated that he was born in the Hellenistic city of Ptolemais Hermii on the Nile in Upper Egypt. He is known to have utilized Babylonian astronomical data. Ptolemy's astronomy and cosmology combined with Aristotle's physics were almost accepted in the West.

The medieval astronomers and cosmologists who wrote in Greek, Arabic, Latin, and Hebrew were all heavily influenced by Ptolemy's theories of cosmology. Ptolemy's cosmology was held in such high regards by cosmologists in Greece, Rome, Arabia, and Egypt.

In 1943, Nicolas Copernicus (1473-1543) wrote a book which set forth his idea of a heliocentric planetary system. The book only composed about 5% of his revolutionary theory. The rest of the book was just a rewrite of Ptolemy's theories. Copernicus hypothesis was that the sun the sun was located at the centre of the universe. This contradicted the theory of Ptolemy in which the earth was at the centre of the universe.

Galileo Galilei (1564 –1642) an Italian physicist, was named the "father of modern observational astronomy". His achievements include improvements to the telescope and consequent astronomical observations, and support for Copernicanism.

Edwin Hubble (1889-1953) was a pioneering American astronomer responsible for several extremely important scientific advances in the early and mid 20th century. By the time of his death in 1953, he was widely regarded as one of the greatest astronomers ever. The Hubble Space Telescope, the most productive space-based telescope in history, is named after him. Hubble's Law, which declares that the further away a galaxy is, the greater a redshift it will have.

- The early theory of earthquakes was that the earth is sitting on a vast ocean, and disturbances in the ocean cause the earth to shake and crack. The ancient Greek belief was that the earthquakes were caused by the anger of the god of the sea (Poseidon), and lighting was the anger of Zeus, the most powerful god on Mount Olympus who made the sun and moon come and go and changed the seasons.

- The Greek Anaximander (611-545 BC) suggested that the earth was a cylinder, and the sun, moon and stars were located on different rings with the same middle point. He further claimed that the stars themselves were rings made of fire. Later, he assumed that all heavenly bodies had previously been regarded as living gods. He also believed that the lower forms of life might be generated by the action of sunlight on moist earth. He also realized that a human baby is not self-sufficient for quite a long time, so suggested that the first humans were born from a certain type of fish.
- The seed theory suggested that the universe was created from a seed which was made from air, water, earth and fire. This theory is similar to the contemporary one in which the universe was created from a singularity point.
- Unfamiliar with tha concept of gravity, Aristotle attributed the idea of objects falling to the ground due to the notion that the earth was located at the center of the univese. The sun was not in the center, because objects fall to the ground.
- The Ptolemaic Cosmological model with the planets and sun moving around the earth as the center of the World. The universe is divided in eight concentric spherical shells, one in which all the stars were fixed, and one for each of the seven planets (Poseidon and Pluto were not known). The sphere of the stars rotates daily around the motionless earth.
- When the first Hubble telescope was in service, it was believed that the Milky Way Galaxy represented the entire universe, and faint objects such as the Andromeda Galaxy were just nebulae similar in size to our own solar system within the Galaxy.

4. Science Background

All objects emit electromagnetic radiation, and the amount of radiation emitted at each wavelength determines the temperature of the object. Hot objects emit more of their light at short wavelengths, and cold objects emit more of their light at long wavelengths. The radiation temperature of an object is related to the wavelength at which the object gives out the most light. We call the amount of light emitted at a particular wavelength, the intensity. When you plot the intensity of light from an object at each wavelength, you trace out a smooth curve called a blackbody curve. For any temperature, the blackbody curve shows how much energy (intensity) is radiated at each wavelength, and the wavelength where the intensity peaks determines the color of that the object. The intensity peak will be at shorter (bluer) wavelengths for hotter objects, and at longer (redder) wavelengths for cooler objects. Therefore, you can tell the temperature of a star or galaxy by its color because color is closely related to the wavelength at which its light intensity peaks.

4.1 Electromagnetic Radiation

Electromagnetic radiation (light waves that are fluctuations of electric and magnetic fields in space) can be described in terms of a stream of photons (photons are generally regarded as particles with zero mass and no electric charge), each traveling in a wave-like pattern, moving at the speed of light (299 792 458 m/s or 186,282 miles/second) and carrying some amount of energy. The spectrum of the electromagnetic radiation usually is divided into seven parts: radio waves, microwaves, infrared, visible, ultraviolet, X-rays and gamma-rays. Cosmic rays are spectrums of higher frequencies than gamma-rays. Table (1) shows the characteristics of above spectrums.

Table (1)

Spectrum	Frequency Range (Hz)	Wave Length	Atomic Transition	Characteristics
Cosmic rays	Above 10^{24}	$>10^{-12}$ m	Hydrogen	High energy range between 10^{13}-10^{16} eV
Gamma rays	10^{20} - 10^{24}	$<10^{-12}$ m	by sub-atomic particle interactions such as electron-positron annihilation, neutral pion decay, radio active decay, fusion and fission in astrophysical process	Unlike optical light and X-rays, gamma rays cannot be captured and reflected in mirrors. The high-energy photons would pass right through such a device
X-rays	10^{17} - 10^{20}	1nm – 1pm	Inner electrons	X-rays are electrically neutral. They

				have neither a positive nor a negative charge. They cannot be accelerated or made to change direction by a magnet or electrical field.
Ultraviolet UV-A (320-420nm), UV-B (280-320 nm), and UV-C (less than 280 nm)	10^{15} -10^{17}	400nm – 1nm	Outer electrons	The cumulative exposure of UV-B radiation may cause sunburn, cataracts, suppressed immune systems, and premature aging including; wrinkles and skin discolorations as well as skin cancer.
Visible	4 - 7.5 x 10^{14}	750nm – 400nm	Outer electrons	Visible light can cause chemical changes in some materials
Infrared	10^{13} - 10^{14}	25μm – 2.5 μm	Outer electrons or molecular vibration	Infrared is used as a powerful tool for determining the internal

				structure of molecules and for identifying the amounts of known species in a given sample
Microwave	$3 \times 10^{11} - 10^{13}$	1mm – 25 µm	Molecular rotations	One of the basic characteristics of microwave energy is that it is reflected by metal
Radio waves	$<3 \times 10^{11}$	>1mm	Molecular spin flip by magnetic filelds	Radio waves move in free space and over the surface of the Earth

Electromagnetic radiation from the universe is unable to reach the surface of the earth except in the visible spectrum, radio frequency, and some ultraviolet wavelengths. Astronomers and astrophysicists use balloons, rocket flights or electromagnetic detectors on orbiting satellites to observe other spectrums. Figure (1) illustrates spectrum wavelength versus altitude.

Figure (1): Spectrum wavelength and altitude

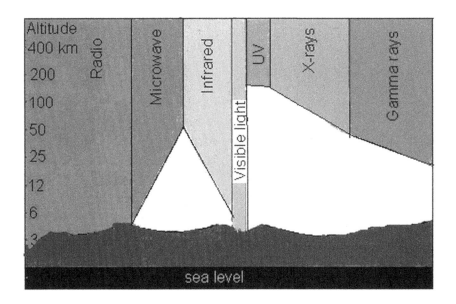

4.2 X-ray Astronomy

X-ray astronomy is part of space science. X-ray emission is expected in sources which contain an extremely hot gas at temperatures from a million to hundred million Kelvin.

In the past three decades, observational astronomy has expanded from the relatively narrow wavelength band of visible light, which is one octave in width (octave is doubling the frequency), to the entire electromagnetic spectrum. Today, more than sixty octaves between the long-wave radio band and the range of high-energetic gamma-ray radiation are used. The mainspring of this development was the awareness that different spectral ranges allow different and complementary insights into cosmic events.

To the most fruitful of these newly opened spectral ranges X-ray astronomy belongs; it covers a band of photon energies between 0.1 keV and 500 keV. The discovery of the first cosmic X-ray source in 1962 came as a surprise. This source is called Scorpius X-1, the first X-ray source found in the constellation Scorpius.

The phenomena which occur at the end of the stellar lifetimes are observable in the X-ray sky. These are called supernova explosions, neutron stars, and black holes. Far outside our own Galaxy, the X-ray sky is dominated by active galaxies (radio galaxies, Seyfert galaxies, and quasars) and by clusters of galaxies, the largest physical formations of our universe. The energy output in X-rays is 100,000 times greater than the total emission of the Sun in all wavelengths.

Normal stars and galaxies, which are comparatively weak X-ray radiators, can be studied with modern X-ray telescopes. And even comets, which pass for "dirty snow balls", are seen in the X-ray sky.

It is now known that such X-ray sources are compact stars, such as neutron stars and black holes. Hot plasmas, with temperatures from a million to a billion degrees, emit X-rays as black body radiation or bremsstrahlung ("braking radiation"). X-ray synchrotron radiation is tangentially produced by the interaction of highly relativistic electrons with cosmic magnetic fields; the inverse Compton effect (the Compton effect is the result of a high-energy photon colliding with a target, which releases loosely bound electrons from the outer shell of the atom or molecule) produces X-rays when highly relativistic electrons interact with intense photon fields.

The celestial sphere has been divided into 88 constellations. The IAU (The International Astronomical Union) constellations are areas of the sky. Each of these contains remarkable X-ray sources. Some of them have been identified from astrophysical modeling to be galaxies or black holes at the centers of galaxies. Some are pulsars, which are rotating neutron stars that emit a beam of electromagnetic radiation.

Surveys of the galaxy in X-rays are designed to help to pin down the structure of the hot gas in our galaxy, but also the interactions occurring at the centre, close to the massive black hole at the Milky Way's core. Flares and prominences on the surface of the Sun also produce X-rays as a result of reconnection of magnetic fields. Large scale surveys help in determining the demographics of some of the X-ray stellar objects, e.g. binaries and cataclysmic variables.

4.3 X-ray Binary System

A binary star is a star system consisting of two stars orbiting around their common center of mass. The brighter star is called the primary and the other is the secondary. A special class of binary stars is the X-ray binaries, so-called because they emit X-rays. X-ray binaries are made up of a primary star and a secondary (a collapsed star such as a white dwarf, neuron star, or black hole). These pairs of stars produce X-rays if the stars are so close together that material is pulled off the normal star by the gravity of the collapsed star, which is denser, Figure (2).

Figure (2): Binary star

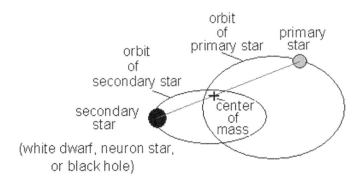

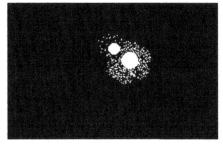

The binary star Albireo (Beta Cygni), which consists
of two stars orbiting around each other every 7,300
years at a mean distance of about 400 billion miles
(650 billion km)

4.4 X-ray Telescopes

Nearly all of the X-ray radiation from cosmic sources is absorbed by the Earth's atmosphere. X-rays have energies in the 0.5 to 5 keV (80 to 800 aJ) range, but can be stopped by a few sheets of paper. Ninety percent of the photons in a beam of three keV (480 aJ) X-rays are absorbed by traveling through just ten cm of air. Even highly energetic X-rays, consisting of photons at energies greater than 30 keV (4,800 aJ), can penetrate through only a few meters of the atmosphere.

Since the minimum altitude for X-ray is about 30km, the X-ray detectors must be flown above most of the Earth's atmosphere. In the past, X-ray detectors were carried by balloons and sounding rockets. Now, scientists prefer to put the detectors on satellites.

The increasing number of galaxy clusters observed with the current generation of X-ray telescopes allows investigators to study the formation and evolution of structure in the universe.

The telescope was introduced to astronomy in 1609 by Galileo. He was able to get magnifications of about 30, with a very narrow field of view. He could only see about ¼ of the Moon's surface at a time. He was first man to see the craters of the moon, sunspots, 4 large moons of Jupiter, rings of Saturn, and the phases of Venus.

Kepler (1611) improved the design of Galileo, Newton invented the Reflecting telescope (1672), William Herschel (1738-1822) then designed huge reflectors and then Bernhard Schmidt (1930) made the Catadiatropic (Catadioptric) Telescope - lenses and mirrors, which is the basic for X-ray telescopes, Figure (3).

Figure (3): Principle of X-rays telescopes (Catadioptric)

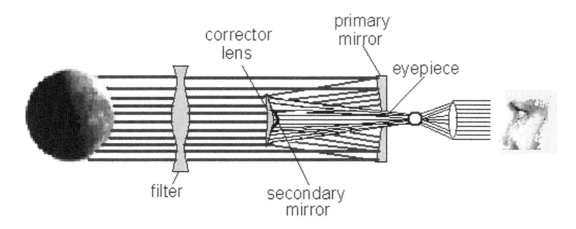

4.5 X-ray Detectors

X-rays, just like any other kind of light, can be thought of as either electromagnetic waves or as massless particles. Measuring X-ray can be accomplished by three methods:

1- Photo-electric absorption in which a photon (e.g. X-ray or gamma ray photon) impinging on an atom transfers its entire energy to an inner shell electron of the atom. The electron is ejected from the atom. The kinetic energy of the ejected photoelectron is equal to the incident X-ray (or gamma ray) photon energy minus the binding energy of the electron, Figure (4). For a given metal and frequency of incident radiation, the rate of energy at which photoelectrons are ejected is directly proportional to the intensity of the incident X-ray.

Figure (4): Photo –electric absorption

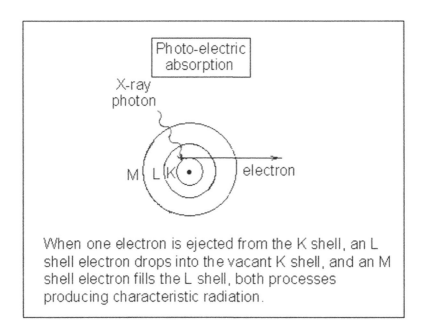

Photo-electric absorption

X-ray photon

M L K • electron

When one electron is ejected from the K shell, an L shell electron drops into the vacant K shell, and an M shell electron fills the L shell, both processes producing characteristic radiation.

4.6 Gamma-Ray and Cosmic Ray Astronomy

Gamma-ray telescopes are designed to observe high-energy astrophysical systems, including stellar coronas, white dwarf stars, neutron stars, black holes, supernova remnants and clusters of galaxies. They also and diffuse gamma-ray background radiation found along the plane of the Milky Way Galaxy.

Gamma rays of cosmic origin extend from an energy of 0.05 MeV (wavelength of 2.5×10^{-11} m) to 10^{11} MeV (10^{-23} m).

Low-energy (or soft) gamma-ray astronomy (up to a few megaelectronvolts) deals mainly with processes in dense media, such as flares, which are associated with magnetars within the Milky Way, and plasmas confined close to neutron stars and black holes.

Gamma-rays are the most energetic form of electromagnetic radiation, with over 10,000 times more energy than visible light photons. By exploring the universe at these high energies, scientists can search for new physics, testing theories and can perform experiments which are not possible in earth-bound laboratories. The penetration power of gamma-ray photons enables the exploration of regions that are hidden at other wavelengths, such as the galactic center region, as well as the first stages of the universe.

Gamma-rays differ considerably from cosmic rays both in characteristics as well as in origin and behaviour. Gamma-rays are photons constituting the most energetic form of electromagnetic radiation. They are photons with the highest frequency and energy of any electromagnetic radiation. Cosmic rays on the other hand, have nothing to do with the electromagnetic radiation. Cosmic rays are in fact high energy charged particles consisting of mainly protons, atomic nuclei, (98%) and electrons (about 2%). Cosmic rays have about 0.1% of their forms as photons of gamma-rays.

Some cosmic rays have energies a billion times greater than those that can be achieved in particle accelerators. In general, most cosmic rays reaching the earth are of lower energy.

Cosmic rays carry electrical charges, and their trajectories are constantly affected by interstellar magnetic fields, making it impossible for astronomers to confirm the directions from which they originate. On the other hand, Gamma-ray photons are neutral and they therefore travel in straight lines and are not affected by magnetic fields. Astronomers can therefore confirm directions from which gamma-rays are coming. While gamma-rays are often accompanied by alpha and beta radiations, cosmic rays are not. Alpha and Beta radiation do not actually involve the emission of electromagnetic radiation, but are instead electrically charged subatomic particles.

Astronomers use gamma-rays to view our Galaxy and beyond, Astroscientists use cosmic rays to deduce useful properties about our Galaxy, such as its composition, its basic structure (is our Galaxy homogeneous? is there an extended halo surrounding our Galaxy?), and what common physical processes occur within the Galaxy (how nuclei accelerate to nearly the speed of light, what kinds of nuclear collisions take place within the interstellar medium, etc). By looking at different properties of cosmic rays, astroscientists learn different things about our Galaxy, much like astronomers use light in different wavelengths to learn about different aspects of the Galaxy.

4.7 Gamma-Ray Telescopes and Detectors

Recent methods to detect gamma-rays use crystal scintillators (semiconductors). Such scintillators emit low energy photons when struck by gamma-rays. These lower energy photons are subsequently collected by photomultiplier tubes, Figure (5). Gamma-rays can create high energy electrons or positrons (e^+) when struck the scintillators. The energy collected can determine the incident gamma-rays. Scintillators are made of inorganic materials such as sodium iodide (NaI) or cesium iodide (CsI). Impurities such as thallium are added to scintillators to activate the interaction.

Inorganic scintillators have been used as gamma-ray detectors aboard many space-based missions to observe sources of cosmic gamma-radiation. Advanced materials such as germanium or the recently popular cadmium zinc telluride (CdZnTe) offer better energy resolution, less noise, and better spatial resolution than the standard scintillators.

Telescopes can either be refracting telescopes, where the light path is bent (refracted) by a lens or reflecting telescopes, where light is reflected off of curved mirrors to a focus. The largest refracting telescope is 1m and the largest reflecting telescope is 10m (largest single mirror is 6m).

Figure (5): Detection of gamma rays

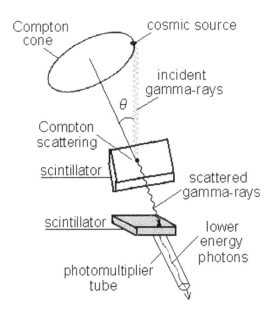

5. Compton Scattering

Compton scattering was first observed by Arthur Compton in 1923 and this discovery led to his award of the 1927 Nobel Prize in Physics. The discovery is important because it demonstrates that light cannot be explained purely as a wave phenomenon, but it can behave as a stream of particles (photons) whose energy is proportional to the frequency.

When the incident photon gives part of its energy to the electron, then the scattered photon has lower energy and, according to the Planck formula, have a lower frequency and a longer wavelength. The wavelength change in such scattering depends only upon the angle of scattering for the target particle of a given material, Figure (6).

Figure (6): Compton scattering

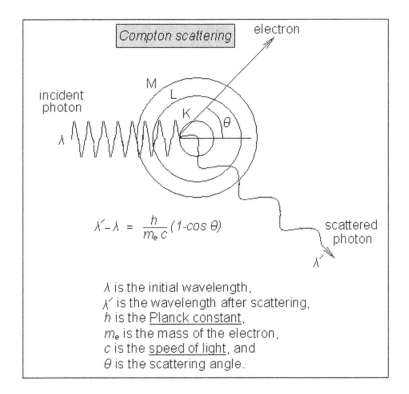

$$\lambda' - \lambda = \frac{h}{m_e c}(1 - \cos\theta)$$

λ is the initial wavelength,
λ' is the wavelength after scattering,
h is the Planck constant,
m_e is the mass of the electron,
c is the speed of light, and
θ is the scattering angle.

The quantity $h/m_e c$ is known as the Compton wavelength of the electron; it is equal to 2.43×10^{-12} m. The wavelength shift $\lambda' - \lambda$ is at least zero (for $\theta = 0°$) and at most twice the Compton wavelength of the electron (for $\theta = 180°$).

6. Rayleigh Scattering

Rayleigh scattering (named after the British physicist Lord Rayleigh) is the scattering of light or other electromagnetic radiation by particles much smaller than the wavelength of the light, such as individual atoms or molecules. Rayleigh scattering is inversely proportional to the fourth power of the wavelength, so that the shorter wavelengths (violet and blue light) will scatter more than the longer wavelengths (yellow and especially red light). Therefore the light scattered down to the earth at a large angle with respect to the direction of the sun's light is predominantly in the blue end of the spectrum. This is the reason for the blue colour of the sky.

Rayleigh scattering can be considered as elastic scattering since the photon energies of the scattered photons is not changed. Scattering in which the scattered photons have either a higher or lower photon energy than the incident photons is called Raman scattering.

Rayleigh scattering occurs when particles are very small. When particles are large such as aerosol' particles, the scattering will be of a forward shape. It is called Mie scattering, Figure (7).

Figure (7): Rayleigh and Mie scattering

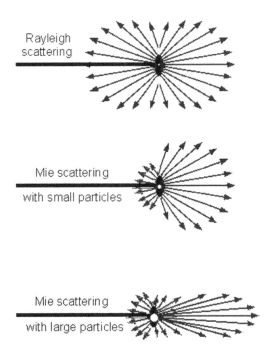

The probability associated with each of these kinds of scattering depends on the energy of the X-ray photon, the bound state the electron is in, and the scattering angle.

7. Light Curves

Light curves are a fundamental tool for variable star astronomy. They are simply a graph of brightness (vertical axis) vs. time (horizontal axis). Figure (8) is a light curve of epsilon Aurigae from its last eclipse.

Figure (8): Light curve of epsilon Aurigae from its last eclipse.

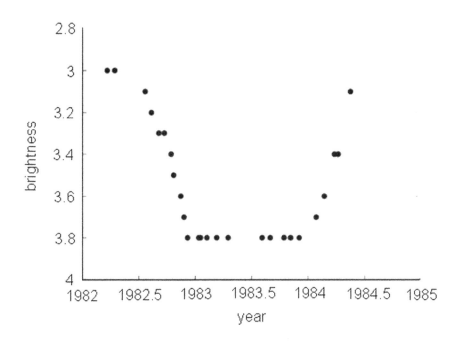

The record of changes in brightness that a light curve provides can help astronomers understand processes at work within the star or stellar system. The curve can identify stellar events through a period of time. For example, the above curve tells us that epsilon Aurigae goes in cycle every three years.

If the light curve looked like Figure (9), scientists would know that this signals the death of a star by a massive explosion called a supernova!

Figure (9): Death of a star

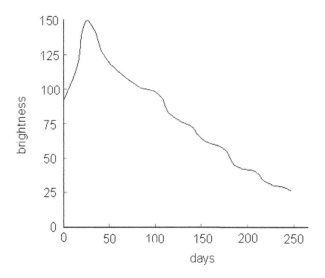

8. Solar System

The following information is provided to give the reader some background about the Solar System and the Galaxy (Milky Way).

The solar system consists of:

- One central star — the Sun
- Eight planets: Mercury, Venus, Earth, Mars, Jupiter, Saturn, Uranus, and Neptune
- More than 160 moons
- Millions of rocky asteroids
- Billions of icy comets

8.1 The Planets

There are eight planets orbiting the sun. In sequence from the sun, the planets are: Mercury, Venus, Earth, Mars, Jupiter, Saturn, Uranus, and Neptune. Pluto was considered the ninth planet until August 2006, when the International Astronomical Union reclassified it as a "dwarf planet". However, in our calculations, it is being considered a planet. See Figure (10)

Figure (10): Planets orbiting the sun - Pluto's inclination is about 17.5 degrees

Sun	center
Mercury	1st
Venus	2nd
Earth	3rd
Mars	4th
Jupiter	5th
Saturn	6th
Uranus	7th
Neptune	8th
Pluto	9th

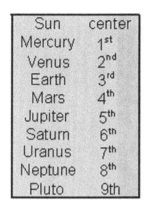
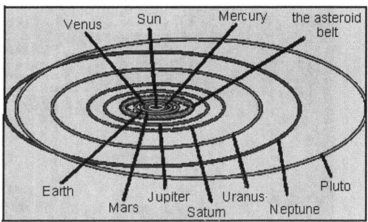

The orbit of Pluto is more elliptical than that of any of the planets (it actually crosses Neptune's orbit). It is tilted at an inclination of 17.15 degrees, relative to the plane of Earth's orbit. The planets all have much smaller inclinations, while objects in the Kuiper Belt (see Fig. 11 below) can have large inclinations like Pluto.

Figure (11): Kuiper Belt with its Elliptical Orbit.

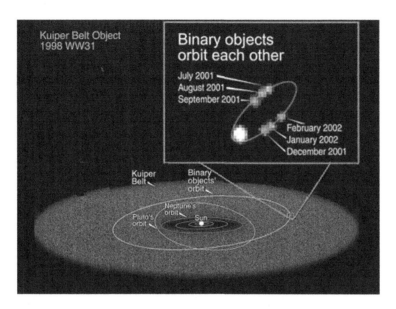

modified from
http://www.ronyerby.com/ss/ssimages/kuiper2%20NASA.jpg

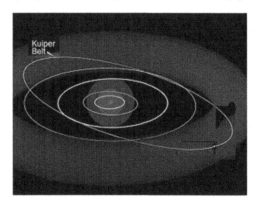

http://upload.wikimedia.org/wikipedia/
commons/9/92/1e12m comparison

Kuiper belt, predicted by Gerard Kuiper in 1950's, is a swarm of icy/rocky objects beyond the orbit of Neptune, between 30 and 50 AU from the sun. Many comets (more than 1000 comets as of 2006) come from the Kulper belt. Kuipler belt was probably formed from leftover objects beyond the orbit of Neptune after the planet formation. Cosmologists don't know much about its evolution.

8.2 Universe Has No Physical Boundaries

In our Galaxy, the Milky Way, there are about 200 billion stars like our sun. Our sun is a very small star compared to other stars. Our sun is called "dwarf sun", but it is the brightest sun. There are subgiant, giant, and supergiant stars. The customary view of the solar system is that it is made up of eight planets orbiting around one star: the sun. Neptune, the farthest planet from the Sun, orbits at approximately 30 astronomical units (AU or 150 million km) from the Sun. An astronomical unit is a unit of length used by astronomers. One astronomical unit equals the average distance from the earth to the sun. The solar system also includes the Kuiper Belt, a comet-rich area that begins near Neptune's orbit and stretches beyond it to about 50 AU from the Sun. Part of Pluto's elliptical orbit stretches far into the Kuiper Belt. Beyond Pluto's orbit is another region of icy objects, called the Oort cloud, which stretches approximately 50,000 AU from the Sun

8.3 The Physical Configuration of Our Planets

Planets come in different sizes and colours. The four planets closest to the Sun are called terrestrial or rocky planets. They are small in size and similar to Earth in composition. Two of them (Earth and Mars) have moons and they have no rings, these four planets are encircled with an "asteroid belt".

The four outer planets, called gas planets, are much larger than the rocky planets. They are giants which all have rings and many moons. The gas giants are made up mostly of hydrogen, helium, frozen water, methane, ammonia, and carbon monoxide.

There is a discussion over whether Pluto is a planet. Some astronomers think that Pluto might be large giant comet). Its composition is similar to that of comets, and its orbit is not parallel to the other planets. Astronomers agree that Pluto is part of the Kuiper Belt of comets because its composition and orbit fit neatly within that group. However, some argue that it should be called a planet as well. Planets are almost circular where comets, asteroids, and objects in Kuiper Built are elliptical. Another belt called the Trojan Belt is located after the Terrestrial Belt, where it coincides with Jupiter.

All belts (Asteroid, Kuiper, and Trojan) are neglected in our calculations because they are very small in mass.

8.4 The Asteroid Belt

The Asteroid Belt is located between the orbits of Mars and Jupiter. Millions of asteroids exist in the Asteroid Belt, with many more scattered throughout the solar system. It is believed that the asteroids in the Asteroid Belt never formed a planet because the gravity of nearby Jupiter, as Mars has no effect, kept pulling them apart.

8.5 Comets

Comets are giant snowballs of ice and rock that formed in the outer space of the solar system, the regions we call the Kuiper Belt and the Oort cloud. When the gravity of a large planet disturbs such a snowball, its orbit can change to pass through the inner solar system. If it passes close enough to the Sun, the ices melt and produce the coma and tail of a comet.

Short-period comets, comets that return to the solar system about once every 100 years, probably originate from the Kuiper Belt. This belt is located within the solar system's ecliptic plane, beyond the orbit of Neptune. Thousands of objects have been discovered in the Kuiper Belt since 1992. These objects are small in comparison with the planets. Their sizes range from 10 to 2500 kilometers in diameter. Earth's diameter, by comparison, is 14,000 kilometers, and therefore they are neglected in the calculation of this study. Astronomers estimate that this belt contains at least 200 million comets.

Long-period comets , comets that we see rarely (once every few thousand years), are thought to born from a vast, spherical cloud of frozen bodies called the Oort Cloud, named for the Dutch astronomer Jan Hendrik Oort. This cloud of comets, which also orbits the sun, is located in the outermost region of the solar system, beyond Neptune and Pluto.

8.6 Planets with Rings

The four gas giants — Jupiter, Saturn, Uranus and Neptune — all have rings. .

8.7 Dwarf Planet

Dwarf planets are small in mass. Astronomers named Ceres, Pluto, and Eris as "dwarf planets". Ceres and Eris are not considered in the coming calculations.

9. The Precession of the Earth's Axis

The Earth's axis rotates (precesses) in a circular shape and the period of precession is about 26,000 years. Therefore, the North Celestial Pole will not always point towards the same domain in the universe. Now the Earth points towards the Polaris Star.
Precession, Figure (12), is caused by the gravitational pull of the sun and the moon on the earth. Precession was discovered by Hipparchus around 130 B.C.

Figure (12): Precession of the Earth

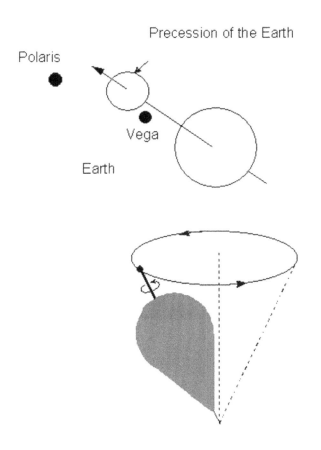

Precession of the Earth

Polaris

Vega

Earth

In 3000 B.C. the north celestial pole coincided with Thuban, a star in the constellation of Draco. Now, the Pole Star in the northern hemisphere is Polaris, In 16,000 A.D. Vega, in Lyra, will be the northern pole star.

In our calculation, the angular momentum of the precession is neglected, as the value is very small compared to angular momentum of other planets.

10. The Galaxy of the Milky Way

The Milky Way has six arms; Norma, Scutum-Crux, Sagittarius, Orion, Perseus, and Cygnus Arm. The sun is in the Orion Arm, which is very close to the centre and is about 90 000 light years in diameter. The Milky Way is about 100, 000 light years in diameter, see Figure (13).

Figure (13): The Milky Way with its six arms. The sun is in the Orion arm.

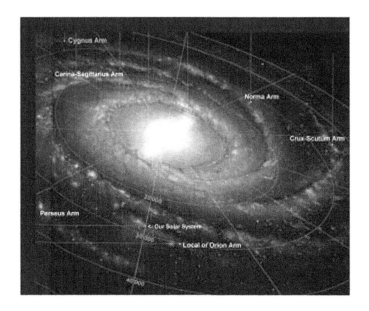

http://www.greatdreams.com/milky_way_arms.jpg

10.1 Properties of the Milky Way

Table (2) shows the properties of the Milky Way (one light year is equal to about ten trillion kilometers). One light year, as defined by the International Astronomical Union is the distance that light travels in a vacuum medium in one Julian year. One Julian year equals 365.25 days.

Table (2): Properties of the Milky Way.

Category of the Milky Way Galaxy	Magnitude
Diameter of the Galaxy	90 000 light years
Number of stars in the Galaxy	200 Billion
Diameter of the Galaxy	25 000 light year
Diameter to the Sun from the centre	26 000 light year
Thickness of the Galaxy at the Sun	2000 light year
Velocity of the Sun around the Galaxy	220 km/second
Year of the Sun around the Galaxy	225 million Earth year
Mass of the Galaxy	1 trillion solar masses

The Sagittarius Galaxy is the nearest galaxy to our own Galaxy, the Orion. Science said that the Sagittarius Galaxy has been 'eaten' by our own galaxy, and therefore, it was named the dwarf Sagittarius galaxy more than a billion years ago. Some galaxies are several thousand light years in size and more than100 000 light years from the centre of our Galaxy. The Andromeda Galaxy is the nearest major Galaxy to the Milky Way (2.2 million light years from it), and has a similar number and configuration of arms as the Milky Way. There are also 100 billions galaxies known to astronomers.

11. Formation of the Solar System Described by Science

The planets, asteroids, and comets in the solar system are free particles left over from the formation of the sun. Planets began to develop and exist as part of the sun. This means that the earth, and all other planets, was developed after the sun .Originally the gas and dust that would become the sun was the core of a cloud much larger than the solar system, probably several light-years across. The core was gradually rotating at first, but as the cloud collapsed it spun faster, like a spinning ice skater pulling in his arms. The start of rotation prevented the material at the core's equator from collapsing as fast as the material at the poles, so the core became a spinning disk.

Gas and dust in the disk spiraled gradually in to the middle, where it accumulated to form the Sun. Because dust is denser than gas, some of the dust settled to the mid-plane of the disk. These dust particles stuck and crushed together to make rocks, then rocks stuck together to make big rocks, and the big rocks collided to make the planets. In the case of the "gas giant" planets (Jupiter, Saturn, Uranus, and Neptune), the rocky cores were massive enough to also attract appreciable amounts of gas. The outer layers of Jupiter and Saturn are made up of hydrogen and other gases. Uranus and Neptune are also "gas giant" planets, but they were built up mainly from ice and dust chunks.

The Sun is the collapsed core of an interstellar gas cloud. The planets, asteroids, and comets are small lumps of dust, ice and rock chunks that stayed in orbit instead of spiraling into the Sun. The planets, including the earth, were formed from a disk left over after the formation of the sun. This disk is called the solar nebula. The nebular hypothesis was mainly developed by Pierre-Simon Laplace.

The planets all formed within a very short period — probably a few million years to about 4.6 billion years ago. The age of the solar system is about 4.6 billion years, which is also the age of the sun.

Planet formation occurred after the formation of the sun. Other theories indicated that the planets formed due to the bulging and an explosion of the sun.

The largest amount of the collapsed cloud collected in the centre, forming the sun, and the rest formed the planets, moons, and asteroids. The sun controls the future of all planets. The accumulation of helium ash at the core of the sun will increase the sun's luminosity and temperature. Consequently, the temperature of the all of planets, including the earth, will increase. This will increase the cycle of the inorganic CO_2, reducing its concentration to deadly levels for plants. Plants will then reduce their output of oxygen, resulting the extinction of animals. This could happen within several million years. After another billion years, all surface water will have vanished. The earth is expected to be effectively habitable for about another 500 million years, but it may live longer than other solar planets. The core of the sun will be cooler than its surface due to the accumulation of helium ash. The sun will expand out to about 250 times its present diameter, and will lose its density and mass. The earth will then move to an orbit 1.7 AU from its present distance from the sun. The sun will become a red giant in about 5 gigayears ($5x10^6$ years), and then convert to a white dwarf, Figure (14). The earth's orbit will become closer to the sun, causing it to enter the red giant Sun's atmosphere and be destroyed.

Figure (14): Life cycle of the sun

The previous outlook on the origin of the universe was forced to change significantly in 1929, when Edwin Hubble discovered that the universe was expanding. Before 1929, the universe was thought to be in a static state. Galaxies and their stars were found to be moving away from each other and from our earth. Scientists started to establish new theories and hypothesis on the creation of the universe.

12. Theories about the Formation of the Universe

Probably the most common theory on this list, the Big Bang gives the Universe an age of 13.7 billion years. However, what caused the Big Bang is still unknown, and there are even more theories that try to explain it, such as the Theory of Everything, or "God started the Big Bang", etc.

Since the 1880's, scientists have observed that light coming from distant stars has a red shift, indicating that those stars are moving away from us at high speeds. In the 1920's Belgian astronomer Georges LeMaître proposed the theory that the universe was created by a huge explosion, and that all the matter in the universe is still flying away from that explosion at enormous speeds. This idea was dubbed the Big Bang Theory by George Gamow circa 1930.

The Big Bang Theory explains why stars in every direction show this red shift. The theory assumed that the Earth is located close to the gravitational center of the universe, which is the presumed site of the Big Bang. So objects speeding away from that explosion will also be speeding away from Earth at roughly the same speed.

There are two theories that can account for both the Big Bang and older objects. The first is the Oscillating Universe theory, namely that the universe periodically expands, then contracts, and explodes again. This would mean that objects older than the Big Bang could have arisen from earlier bangs. The second is the Many Bang theory, namely that the Big Bang is just one of many bangs at many sites, and the objects could have originated at any of many different sites and times.

Therefore, we need to find a framework that accommodates the older and the recent (13.7 billion years) objects.

Without any evidence associated with the earliest instant of the expansion, the Big Bang theory cannot and does not provide any explanation for such an initial condition; rather, it describes and explains the general evolution of the universe since that instant.

There are, however, several things that the Big Bang Theory does not explain, such as the distribution of matter in the universe, pulsars, the apparent lack of anti-matter, the lack of sufficient mass to hold galaxies together, the seeming acceleration in the rate the universe is expanding, and the discovery of objects that are apparently older than the Big Bang.

12.1 The Creation of the Big Bang Theory

If you go back in time and reverse the expansion, you will find that the galaxies come closer together, and the universe becomes smaller, hotter, and denser. If you go back in time far enough, you will find that all the galaxies, stars and every thing in the universe, are compressed into a tiny, infinitely hot and dense place called a singularity. In 1930, after the discovery of Edwin Hubble, cosmologists started to look for new theories; one of them is the Big Bang Theory. Cosmologists tried to formulate new theories on how the universe began. In the 1930's, soon after Edwin Hubble's discovery, cosmologists first established what is now known as the Big Bang Theory. The theory states that the universe began with a major explosion at the point of singularity, which caused all the matter in the universe (in the form of hot gases and particles), to expand evenly throughout space. The gas moved away from the center of the singularity point, much like debris from an explosion. As the gases and particles expanded, it cooled and become dense, allowing the formation of the planets, stars and galaxies.

The Big Bang Theory predicted that galaxies should be moving apart, just as Edwin Hubble suggested. The theory soon became popular and acknowledged as the standard universe-creation theory. However, the Big Bang theory can not explain:

- The location of the singularity point, and how it started
- The density and the mass of the singularity point to construct this huge universe
- The Big Bang Theory talked about things that occurred after the Big Bang, but not before or during its occurrence.
- The explosion of the singularity point should have made the universe identical and harmonized.

Although the Big Bang Theory made some predictions that corresponded with some observations and discoveries, the theory left many things to be explained and improved.

12.2 The Big Crunch

Gravity is the force of attraction between particles of matter. The amount of gravitational force one object exerts on another depends upon the size of the two objects and the distance between them. If there's enough matter in the universe, the force of gravity will eventually slow the expansion and cause the universe to contract. Eventually the entire universe will contract and collapse in on itself. Cosmologists call this the Big Crunch. Some theorize that our universe is just the latest in a series of universes generated in a cycle of space expanding and contracting.

Eventually all of the matter in the Universe will collapse into a super dense state and possibly even collapse into an unimaginably massive black hole. Some theorize that the Universe could collapse into the same state that it began as and then blow up in another Big Bang. In this way the Universe would last forever but would continually go through these phases of expansion and contraction, Big Bang and Big Crunch and so on...

The end of the universe would then resemble its beginning—a singularity at which the laws of physics as we know them no longer apply. Such a universe is called a closed universe.

12.3 The Bouncing Universe

This theory was established in 1960 in which the universe come into being through the so called "Bug-Bang" emerged from something similar to the singularity point, expanded for a while and then implode and then bounced to explode in a new Big Bang. That is why the universe is following a wave of expansions and contractions.

Some universe theorists suggest that the universe started by the so called Big Bang, and after the period of expansion, went into the period of contraction. So, the universe derives from the cyclic pattern or oscillatory universe interpretation of the Big Bang, where the first cosmological event was the result of the collapse of a previous universe. In other words, the universe passed through a cycle started either by the Big Bang or the Big Crunch and ends with the Big Crunch or the Big Bang respectively, or more simply, a Big Bounce. So, the question is where is our recent universe standing in the cycle? Is it the first, tenth or billionth universe? Or the last universe? Theorists have an imagination of the Big Bounce as depicted in Figure (15).

Figure (15): The Big Bounce Cycle

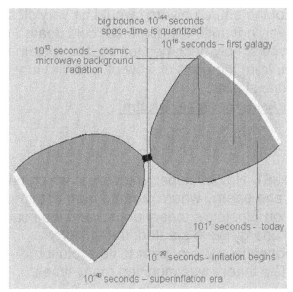

Big Bounce Theory grew from the collapse of pre-existing universe that bounce back from its symmetrical in time around the moment of maximum compression.

12.4 The Big Rip (Finite Lifespan)

The Big Rip suggests that in the future of our continually expanding universe, the dark energy, a hypothetical form of energy against the gravity, increases (it will have more negative pressure than a simple cosmological constant) and causes the expansion of the universe to accelerate with time. The universe will then reach a state where it is impossible for any life to exist. As a result, all material objects in the universe, starting with galaxies and eventually (in a finite time) all forms, no matter how small, will disintegrate into the elementary particles. The end would be that the universe continues to exist, but as a murky gas of photons, leptons and protons, growing less dense as time goes on.

12.5 The Big Freeze or Heat Death

The Big Freeze (Heat Death) occurs when no heat is transferred from one object to another. The energy (the heat) from the instant of the Big Bang will be distributed in the universe until it reaches a steady value. This means that the entropy will reach its maximum value and the heat system will evenly distribute. At this point, no thermodynamic free energy to sustain motion or life is possible.

This conclusion is a contrast to the Big Crunch which is characterized by a collapse of unimaginably gargantuan proportions and will eventually culminate into an immensely massive black hole. This Big Freeze will wind down to a cold silent halt.

In a "Heat Death", the temperature of the entire universe would be very close to absolute zero. Heat Death is, however, not quite the same as "cold death", or the "Big Freeze", in which the universe simply becomes too cold to sustain life due to continued expansion; though, from the point of view of anything that could observe either, the result is quite similar, [http://www.physlink.com/Education/AskExperts/ae181.cfm].

12.6 The Inflationary Theory

Alan Guth postulated his theory in 1981. He developed a theory in which he states that large amounts of matter and energy where created from nothing. The nothingness theory was based on Einstein's theory $e=mc^2$ and the scalar field of energy. After the matter and energy were created, the universe accelerated its expansion in an exponential pattern, prior to its evolution, according to the Big Bang Theory. The theory was modified many times.

12.7 The Protouniverse Theory

This theory is similar to the nothingness theory, and it is sometimes called "the white hole theory". A white hole is the opposite of a black hole. The black hole absorbs light, and the white hole emits light, where matter would continuously appear as a light. This theory was probably formulated in an attempt to point out the non-uniformity and the varying density and mass of the universe.

12.8 The Bubble Universe

The Bubble Universe Theory suggested that universes were created from very small foams (quantum foams) of a "parent universe". The quantum foams were created from fluctuations of energy which created small bubbles. These bubbles expanded and contracted, and then disappeared. When the energy fluctuation was greater than a critical value, the small bubbles created the universe from the parent universe. Within the new universe however, if the energy fluctuation was greater than a particular critical value, a tiny bubble universe forms from the parent universe. It goes through continuing expansion, and allows matter and large-scale galactic structures to form.

12.9 Andre Linde's Self Creating Universe

The Andre Linde's self-creating universe theory suggested that bubbles of the above theory were developing other bubble universes which in turn developed other bubble universes. Our universe was modified for the evolution of life.

12.10 The Hawking-Turok Instanton Theory

The Hawking-Turok Instanton Theory suggested that the universe was created from nothingness. The universe was created spontaneously form an open, inflationary bubble through explosion and implosion processes.

12.11 The Hartle and Hawking No-Boundary Theory

The Hartle and Hawking No-Boundary Theory suggested that there should be many universes based on a superset theory encompassing general relativity and quantum mechanics. The theory also suggested that universes had no boundaries. Wave functions are based on quantum particles such, as electrons and positrons which can be in various waves. High waves represent our universe, and small waves represent other small universes. The theory considered the universes as quantum particles that we shall discuss later. Universes based on the quantum theory (wave functions) are shown in Figure (16).

Figure (16): Universes and quantum theory (wave functions)

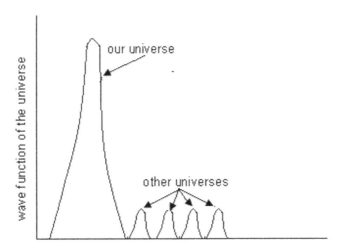

Hartle and Hawkins suggested that the universe is an open curvature like a horse saddle which curves down on one side and curves up on the other, Figure (17). Thus, the universe expands faster than the inflationary theory, and will continue to expand.

Figure (17): A saddle – shaped universe

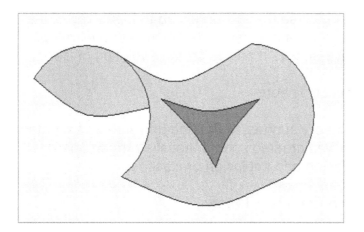

Small waves and large waves of the Hartle and Hawking No-Boundary Theory can be represented by a cone shape of the space–time module with its tip pointing downwards. Time represents the vertical axis and space represents the horizontal axis. The time and space meet together at the tip, or at singularity. At the tip all mathematical equations of the laws of physics break down because no parameters exist there, except 0, 0, 0, and 0, which cannot be defined in the four dimensions a space, Figure (18).

Figure (18): A Conic shaped universe

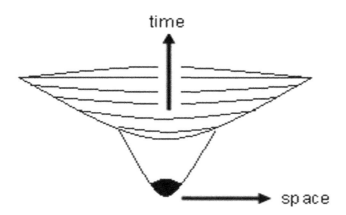

12.12 Oscillatory universe

The oscillatory universe theory is an astrophysical model investigated briefly by Albert Einstein in 1930 and critiqued by Richard Tolman in 1934, in which the universe undergoes a series of oscillations, each beginning with a Big Bang and ending with a Big Crunch. After the Big Bang, the universe expands for a while before the gravitational attraction of matter causes it to collapse back in and undergo a bounce, http://en.wikipedia.org/wiki/Oscillatory_universe.

Tolman predicts that the universe may grow cold and dark and ultimately end frm over-heart. The death can happen if the universe expands for ever and if the universe is flat or open. Alternatively, if the universe is closed, the expansion will eventually stop, and the universe will begin to contract once expansion stops. The contraction would be very slow at first and then accelerate and grow hotter and brighter until it ends in the Big Crunch. The universe then implodes into singularity and becomes out of existence.

However, some cosmologists think that the universe would not extinct; they assume that another Big Bang would follow the singularity point (the Big Crunch). The cycle from singularity to another Big Bang back to the singularity point would never end. The cycle is known as an oscillating universe.

13. Sequence of the Formation of the Universe

Cosmologists can not fully comprehend the exact process from which our universe was formed. However, there are numerous theories as to how it may have bee born. The most commonly accepted theory today is the Big Bang theory that proposed in the 1920's and 1930's. The sequence of the formation of the universe as proposed by cosmologists is:

13.1 The Big Bang Stage

The Big Bang started 13.7 billion years ago when the universe had no time and no space. As per NASA, 300 thousand years after the Big Bang, hydrogen nuclei captured electrons, forming the first atoms. Formation of first galaxies started 600 million years after the Big Bang. Our sun formed before 4.5 billion years ago, and was followed by the formation of the earth and our planets.

The Big Bang started at 0 seconds (assume there was no time), and at an infinite temperature. (Kelvin temperature at a very high temperature equals centigrade temperature).

There are several theories about the formation and the ultimate fate of the universe. The best available theory as of 2010 suggests that the evolution of the universe is divided into three phases:

1. The very early universe was so hot that particles had energies higher than those currently accessible in particle accelerators on Earth.

2. In the second phase, protons, electrons and neutrons were formed, then finally the atoms with their nuclei. In this phase, the atom of hydrogen was formed, and then the cosmic microwave was emitted.

3. Matter then continued to accumulate into the first stars and ultimately galaxies, quasars, clusters of galaxies and superclusters formed.

13.2 The Steady State Theory

There are many scientists who oppose the Big Bang theory. The Steady State Theory (proposed in the late 1940's) is a concept developed to fill the holes left in the Big Bang Theory.

The Steady State Theory proposes that matter is being continuously created, at the rate of roughly one hydrogen atom per cubic meter per billion years. This probably equals the rate of a few hundred atoms per year. The continuous creation of matter is needed to keep the density of the universe constant as it expands. This violates the first law of thermodynamics, but then again, so does the Big Bang Theory. The violation is represented in the continuous increase in the temperature of the universe. Therefore, if the Big Bang Theory and the Steady State Theory are acceptable, the universe will destroy itself due to the continuous increase in its temperature.

There was another doubt shed on the Steady State Theory when scientists discovered the cosmic background radiation. Cosmic background radiation proved that the universe is accelerating. The acceleration of the universe has added another uncertainty to the Big Bang Theory. The doubt on both theories has led scientists to look at them the wrong way. Scientists don't really know how the origin of the universe happened.

14. The Cosmic Microwave Background Radiation

The cosmic microwave background radiation (CMBR) is a form of electromagnetic radiation filling the universe. When we look to the universe through an optical telescope, the space between stars and galaxies is pitch black, but when we use a radio telescope, there is a faint background glow of the same brightness in all directions. However, it is not associated with any star, galaxy, or other stellar body. This glow is highest in the microwave region, hence the name Cosmic Microwave Background Radiation.

The highly isotropic (same in all directions) nature of the cosmic background radiation indicates that the early stages of the universe were almost completely uniform. This raises three problems for the Big Bang theory.

First, when we look at the microwave background coming from widely separated parts of the sky it can be shown that these regions are too separated to have been able to communicate with each other even with signals traveling at light velocity. Thus, how did they know to have almost exactly the same temperature? This general problem is called the Horizon Problem. Contrary to this expectation, the universe is in fact extremely homogeneous. For instance, the cosmic microwave background radiation (CMBR), which fills the universe, is almost precisely the same temperature everywhere in the sky, about 2.725 K. This presents a serious problem; if the universe had started with even slightly different temperatures in different areas, then there would simply be no way it could have evened itself out to a common temperature by this point in time.

Without any evidence associated with the earliest instant of the expansion, the Big Bang theory cannot and does not provide any explanation for such an initial condition; rather, it describes and explains the general evolution of the universe since that instant.

Calculation:

Assume the CMBR is traveling through our galaxy (the Milky Way) at light velocity. Considering our galaxy is a diameter of 100,000 light years, the period required for the CMBR to travel from one end to the other (by this point in time) is about 9.5×10^8 billion years. The Big Bang happened before 13.7 billion years. Therefore, the CMBR contradicts the Big Bang Theory.

The present universe is homogenous and isotropic, but only on very large scales. For scales of the size of superclusters and smaller than the luminous matter, the universe is quite lumpy, as suggested by scientists. Therefore, the CMBR should be anisotropic. One of the wide ranges of theories attempting to explain the origin of the Universe was eventually discredited and superseded by the Big Bang hypothesis based upon the cosmic microwave background radiation which is seen as isotropic waves.

The theory of the Big Bang stated that the temperature and the corresponding time were as shown in Table (3).

Table (3): Temperature and time as suggested by the Big Bang Theory

	Temperature, K°	Corresponding time
1	100 billion	0.1 seconds
2	10 billion	1 second
3	3 billion	13.8 seconds
4	1 billion	3 minutes and 45 seconds
5	3 million	35 minutes
6	Several thousands	700,000 years
7	3.7 (CMBR)	13.7 billion years

Let's look to the graph's corresponding data up to rows 5, 6, and 7 which are shown in Figure (19).

Figure (19): Graphs corresponding data up to rows 5, 6, and 7 of above table

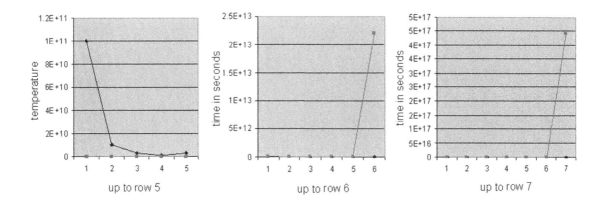

From the right graph we can see the temperature increased. This means that the universe stopped from the expansion state (or contracted). This occurred 35 minutes from the Big Bang occurrence.

Between 35 minutes and 700,000 years (see the table), the temperature decreased 0.23 $K°$ each year. It decreased 3×10^{-7} $K°$ per year from 700,000 years to 13.7 billion years. The temperature shift in the right and the middle graph is not shown because of the huge difference in temperature between the two periods. This dramatic shift in temperature would explain that the red shift is due to the Compton effect (because at higher temperatures, electrons move away from the nucleus of the atom, and therefore, the energy of the input gamma ray equals the energy of the output gamma ray plus the bonding energy of the driven electrons. Also, the total intensity radiated over all wavelengths increases as the temperature increases as I equals αT^4, α is the Stefan-Boltzmann constant) rather than Doppler Effect. Therefore, the Big Bang Theory is doubtful.

15. Density Parameter

The density parameter (Ω) is the ratio of the actual mean density of mass-energy in the universe (ρ) to the critical density (ρ_c). The relationship as identified by Friedman is:

$\Omega = \rho/\rho_c$

So, the eternal shape of the universe would be one of the following, Figure (20):

Spherical shape (closed universe) when Ω is greater than 1, open universe (like that of the surface of saddle) when Ω is less than 1, or flat universe when Ω is close to 1

Figure (20) Eternal shape of the universe

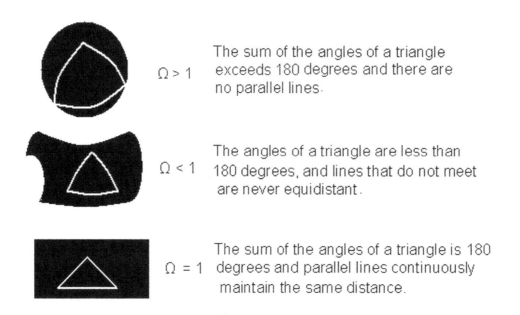

$\Omega > 1$ The sum of the angles of a triangle exceeds 180 degrees and there are no parallel lines.

$\Omega < 1$ The angles of a triangle are less than 180 degrees, and lines that do not meet are never equidistant.

$\Omega = 1$ The sum of the angles of a triangle is 180 degrees and parallel lines continuously maintain the same distance.

The critical density (ρ_c) is the average density of matter in the universe today that would be needed to halt, at some point in the future, the cosmic expansion. A universe that has precisely the critical density is said to be flat or Euclidean. To date, the critical density is estimated to be approximately five atoms (of monatomic hydrogen) per cubic meter, whereas the average density of ordinary matter in the Universe is believed to be 0.2 atoms per cubic meter.

The critical density would reach its maximum value because of the dark energy which would lead to the expansion of the universe, and also lead to the acceleration of its expansion.

Scientists who don't support the Big Bang theory raised questions on the ultimate fate of the universe. Is it when Ω becomes less than 1, equals 1, or larger then 1. This would depend upon the physical properties of the mass/energy of matter in the universe, its average density, and the rate of expansion.

Einstein formulated his general relativity theory based on two things: the idea that the universe is static and the idea that the cosmological constant can be allowed for the expansion and the contraction of the universe. After Hubble announced his conclusion that the universe was expanding (not static), Einstein wrote that his cosmological constant was "the greatest blunder of my life".

16. Repulsive Force

Recently, the Wilkinson Microwave Anisotropy Probe (WMAP) spacecraft has indicates that the universe is close to flat, i.e. Ω is close to 1. This means the mass/energy density of the universe must be equal to a certain critical density. But measurement of the cosmic microwave background indicates that the total amount of matter in the universe is only about 30% of the critical density. The question is, where is the remaining density which accounts for 70%? The answer is the dark energy. This is consistent with the theoretical calculation that the universe is made of 74% dark energy, 22% dark matter, and 4% ordinary matter, [Hinshaw, Gary F. (April 30th, 2008). "WMAP Cosmological Parameters Model: lcdm+sz+lens Data: wmap5"]. The composition of the universe is shown in Figure (21).

Figure (21): The composition of the universe

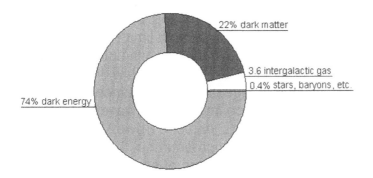

Dark energy is the most popular way to explain recent observations and experiments that the universe appears to be expanding at an acceleration rate.

In 1998, cosmologists were shaken by the discovery that the universe is expanding at an astonishing rate. This was proven by the fast escape of the supernova type 1a. There are some non-believers, with good cause. Some say these most distant supernovae may just look far (that is, dim) because intervening dust scatters their light. Also, we cannot be certain that the most distant supernovae explode in the same way as closer ones.

The question was simply whether or not the expansion would slowly come to a halt and bring the universe falling back in the 'Big Crunch'. This could be true if there is enough matter in the universe, then the gravity could halt and bring it into the Big Crunch. But there is not enough matter (above Figure) to create such a huge gravity. Thus, scientists believe that there is another force, called the repulsive force, which causes the universe to expand.

Einstein admitted that he made a big mistake when he added a factor called the cosmological constant to compensate for his thought that the universe was static (stand still). The cosmological constant was an anti-gravity 'vacuum' force that kept gravity from pulling the universe in on itself. By 1930, Edwin Hubble discovered that the Milky Way was but one of a multitude of galaxies and that the universe was expanding. So, there was no longer a need for a cosmological constant.

It is now believed that the force making the universe expand is the repulsive force (which could be due to the dark energy). Scientists believe that the dark energy was much smaller in a young universe than the attractive gravitational force. With increasing time and distance the dark repulsive force increased and became greater than the gravitational attraction. If this is true, that the repulsive force is increased, no body knows whether it increased linearly, exponentially, or randomly.

17. Quantum Cosmology

The quantum cosmology developed by Hawking and his collaborators gives an unconditional probability for the existence of our universe. The word quantum applies to the infinitesimally small world of quarks and leptons (will be explained later), while cosmology signifies the almost limitless expanse of outer space. However, many scientists now believe that the ultimate questions of cosmology can be answered only by quantum physics. Hawking takes quantum cosmology to its ultimate conclusion, suggesting the existence of infinite numbers of parallel universes. Quantum cosmology is a wave function that describes all the various possible states of a particle. However, it cannot describe the position of an electron and its momentum in the same time, thus leading to the uncertainty of the physical structure of an electron or a particle. If Hawking found parallel universes from his calculations, this would mean that the starting point of Hawking's theory must be an infinite set of parallel universes of uniform feature of waves. In his analysis, he replaced the word particle with universe, considering the particle as a photon of certain a wave shape. At this stage (quantum cosmology), electrons did not even exist, thus, the atom did not exist (note that atoms consist of protons, neutrons, and electrons). However, matter and antimatter existed in 51% to 49 % respectively, but they did not have any influence on the formation of the universe because they were dominated by the energy of the universe.

17.1 Quarks and Leptons Stage

After some seconds, the universe had cooled to about 10^{28} K. and it was cool enough for particles (baryogenesis) which are the building blocks for atom formation. Protons and neutrons were then formed at 10^{24}K(one proton has two up quarks and one down quark, and one neutron has one up quark and two down quarks). At this stage, where the temperature is 10^{28}K, the universe was still too hot to form protons and neutrons. So at this temperature (10^{28}k), only quarks were existed.

17.2 The Inflation Stage

At about 10^{20}K, the universe experienced a period of very rapid inflation and expanded very quickly which is known as the inflation stage. The universe inflated from a tiny particle smaller than the nucleus of an atom (10^{-25} meters) to a universe of a depth of about 1 billion light-years (10^{+25} meters). Our galaxy has a diameter of about 100,000 light year. This inflation was the cause of the strong nuclear force from the electroweak force.

17.3 The Hadrons Stage

The universe had cooled to 10^{13} K and electrons and neutrinos (leptons) were formed in huge numbers. Baryons (hadrons) and mesons were formed (one baryon has 3 quarks, and one meson has two quarks or one quark and one antiquark). Atoms were still not formed as 10^{13}K was too hot for their formation. The combination of quarks needed a strong force "gluons" which could not be structured at a high temperature.

17.4 Atomic Nuclei Stage

The universe had cooled to approximately 10^{10}K (1000 times hotter than the temperature of the core of the sun). Protons and neutrons were formed at a ratio of p:n = 1:0.223, i.e. every 100 protons, and there were 22.3 neutrons. The ratio did not stay stable as many neutrons decayed to beta rays and converted to protons with a half-life of 600 seconds.

17.5 Recombination Stage

As the universe expands and cools, protons and electrons combine to form hydrogen (the most abundant element). Helium nuclei then combine with electrons to from helium atoms. This process is called recombination.

The above stages are shown in Figure (22).

Figure (22): Important stages of the formation of the universe

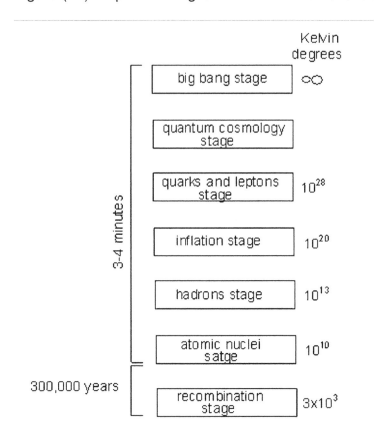

The formation of the universe passed through three eras: the lepton era, the radiation era, and the matter era, Figure (23). The density (gram per cubic centimeter) of the universe in each era is different and varies with time. The density in the lepton and radiation eras is proportional to the square of time, i.e. $d= c x 1/t^2$, c is a constant, and t is the age of the universe at that point. It means that an increase in age by a factor of 10 reduces the density by a factor of 1/100. In the matter era, density is proportional to T^3, where T is the temperature of the cosmic radiation. In this era, T is proportional to $t^{-2/3}$.

Figure (23): The three eras and densities of the universe

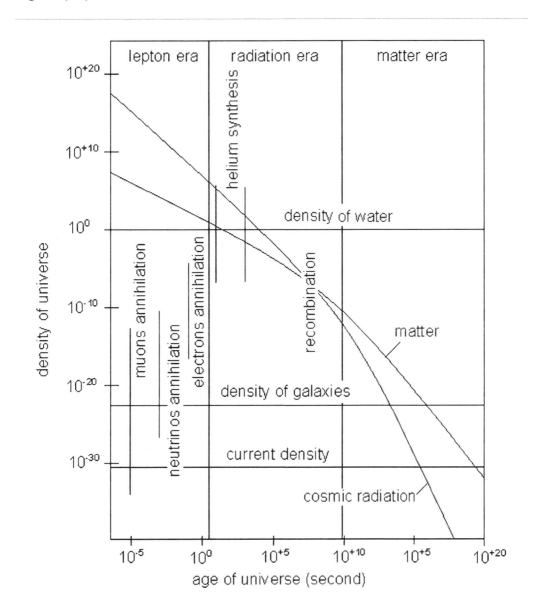

18. Atomic Decays

Radioactive decay is the process by which an atomic nucleus of an unstable atom loses energy by emitting ionizing particles (ionizing radiation).

In order to produce a more stable nucleus, process of disintegration should be undergone by the nuclei of radioactive elements, such as radium and various isotopes of uranium and the transuranic elements, The three most common forms of radioactive decay are alpha, beta, and gamma decay.

18.1 Alpha Decay

In Alpha Decay, the nucleus emits an atom of helium ($^4H2$), which is an alpha particle. Alpha Decay occurs most often in massive nuclei that have too large a proton to neutron ratio such as uranium, ($^{238}U92$). An alpha particle, with its two protons and two neutrons, is a very stable configuration of particles. Alpha radiation reduces the ratio of protons to neutrons in the parent nucleus, bringing it to a more stable configuration. Thus, uranium can be decayed to thorium ($^{234}Th90$), as shown in Figure (24).

Figure (24): Alpha decay

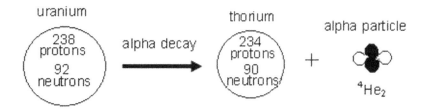

In Alpha Decay, the atomic number changes, so the original (or parent) atoms and the decay-product (or daughter) atoms are different elements, as seen from Figure (6).Therefore, they have different chemical and physical properties. Because the daughter (thorium) has a smaller mass, most of the kinetic energy goes to the alpha particle.

18.2 Beta Decay

Beta particles are electrons or antielectrons. Antielectrons are called positrons (electrons with positive electric charge). Beta decay occurs when an atom has a nucleus with too many protons or too many neutrons; one of the protons or neutrons is transformed into the other. In a nucleus with too many neutrons, the protons try to be in balance with neutrons. Thus, neutrons loose some of their balanced charge in order to convert into protons, and vice versa. In Beta Minus Decay, a neutron decays into a proton, an electron, and an antineutrino:

Beta Minus equation

$$n \longrightarrow p + e^- + \bar{\nu}^-$$

To balance the equation in terms of leptons, n = 0 lepton, p = 0 lepton, electron = 1 lepton, antineutrino = -1.

In Beta Plus Decay, a proton decays into a neutron, a positron, and a neutrino:

Beta plus equation

$$p \longrightarrow n + e + \nu$$

To balance the equation in terms of leptons, p = 0 lepton, n = 0 lepton, positron e = -1 lepton, antineutrino = 1.

Leptons are created at the instant of the decay, they are not present in the nucleus before the decay.

A hydrogen atom has an isolated proton with or without an electron, and does not decay. However, the Beta Decay (at very high temperature) can change a proton to a neutron. Also, an isolated neutron is unstable and can be changed to a proton in a half-life of10.5 minutes which depends on the isotope (a isotope is a nuclide with the same atomic number but a different atomic mass. A nuclide means an atom. A proton may capture an electron and can change to a neutron and a neutrino. So, the process of Beta Decay involves three transitions; proton decay, neutron decay, and electron capture, or vice versa. In each Beta Plus Decay, parents and daughters are different elements. They have the same number of protons and a different number of neutrons which increase or decrease by 2, and vise versa with Beta Minus. Note that Beta Decay can convert the mass into energy, and vice versa. Hydrogen decay needs a high temperature to emit beta particles. The high temperature can be produced when hydrogen protons collide or annihilate after which the energy is converted into mass. It was proposed that this happened at the first instant of the formation of the universe.

18.3 Gamma Rays

Gamma Rays are electromagnetic radiation of high energy, above100 keV (kilo electron volt) and have frequencies above 10^{19} Hz (cycle per second) with wavelength less than 10 picometers (10×10^{-12} meter). Gamma Rays cause serious damage to human tissues, and are a health hazard. For example, carbon can emit Gamma Rays and produce nitrogen if the carbon atom is hit with hydrogen, and nitrogen can emit Gamma Rays and produce oxygen if the nitrogen atom is hit by hydrogen, Figure (25).Figure (25): Annihilation of hydrogen and elements to produce gamma rays and different elements

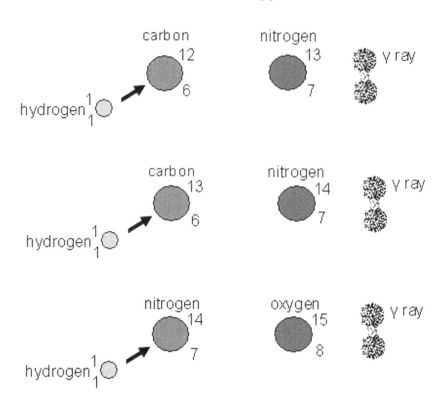

Gamma rays are the smallest wavelengths and have the most energy of any other electromagnetic wave spectrums. Gamma rays are produced when radioactive atoms decay and also in nuclear explosions. They are very dangerous and can kill living cells and cancerous cells. Gamma rays are used in medicine to kill tumor cells when patients are treated by radioactivity. Wavelengths of electromagnetic waves, including Gamma rays are shown in Figure (26).

Figure (26): Gamma rays and other electromagnetic waves

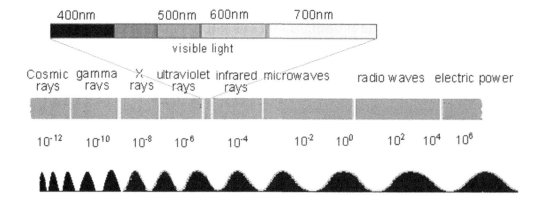

Gamma-rays travel to the earth across cosmic distances of the universe, only to be absorbed by the Earth's atmosphere. Different wavelengths of light infiltrate the Earth's atmosphere to different depths. Gamma-rays are the most active form of light and are produced by the hottest solid areas of the universe. They are also produced by powerful supernova (massive stars die) explosions, the destruction of atoms, and the decay of radioactive material in space. Gamma rays are also produced by neutron stars, pulsars, and black holes. Gamma rays cannot be detected on the surface of the earth. Balloons or space craft above the atmosphere, carrying Gamma ray telescope can only detect gamma rays. Gamma ray telescopes use a special technique called Compton Scattering (the discoverer was Arthur Compton, 1923) process, where Gamma rays strike an electron and lose energy.

Gamma ray bursts are the name given to flashes of Gamma rays emanating at random from distant galaxies. They are the most radiant electromagnetic fields in the universe after the occurrence of the Big Bang. Their duration is typically a few seconds and they can release more energy in 10 seconds than the sun will emit in its entire 10 billion-year lifetime! So far, it appears that all of the bursts we have observed have come from outside the Milky Way Galaxy. By solving the mystery of Gamma ray bursts, scientists hope to gain more knowledge of the origins of the universe, the rate at which the universe is expanding, the size of the universe and whether the universe has multi layers of spiral shape as proposed by Stephen Hawking.

19. The Building Blocks of Matter

19.1 Atomic Structure

Atoms are made up of 3 types of particles electrons, protons, and neutrons. Electrons are very small and light particles that have negative charges. Protons are much larger and heavier than electrons and have positive charge. Neutrons are large and slightly heavier than protons, and have no electrical charges, Figure (27).

Figure (27): Atomic structure

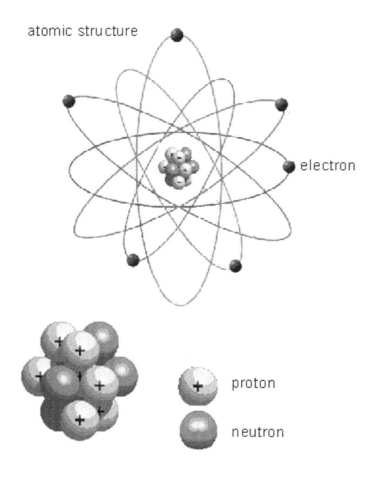

Today, scientists have proved theoretically and experimentally that the protons and neutrons are made up of even smaller particles, called quarks. Particles that cannot be broken further such as quarks are sometimes called fundamental particles.

Scientists now believe that the nucleus of an atom (nucleus has only protons and neutrons) has protons and neutrons made of smaller particles: quarks and three other types of particles—leptons, force-carrying bosons, and the Higgs boson—which are truly fundamental and cannot be split into anything smaller. Higgs bosons have not yet been proven experimentally. In the 1960s American physicists Steven Weinberg and Sheldon Glashow and Pakistani physicist Abdus Salam (they shared the Noble prize for their discovery), developed a mathematical description of the nature and behavior of elementary particles. The term elementary particles has the same meaning as fundamental particles but is used more loosely to include some subatomic particles that are composed of other particles.Their theory, known as the Standard Model of Particle Physics, has greatly advanced the understanding of the fundamental particles and forces in the universe. Some questions about particles, including

Boson particles, remain unanswered by the standard model, and physicists continue to develop a theory that will explain even more about many particles emitted from the universe.

Atoms can be classified into one of the two categories called Fermions or Bosons. Fermions are fundamental particles forming protons and neutrons. Fundamental bosons carry forces between particles and give particles mass, Figure (28).

It was proven by Wolfgang Pauli, an Austrian American, that no two electrons have the same momentum and location. This was called the Exclusion Principle. The Exclusion Principle was developed to include all particles that obey such a principle. Fermions, in honour of the Italian American physicist Enrico Fermi, which include quarks and leptons, obey the Exclusion Principle theory.

German American physicist and an Indian mathematician Satyendra Bose proved that Bosons (see Figure (28) below), suggested that they did not obey the Exclusion Principle. Bosons, in honor of Bose, include photons, gluons, and weak forces. Higgs bosons were proven theoretically, but not yet experimentally.

The Exclusion Principle can be based on the number of fermions. If the number of fermions is even, then the atom does not obey the Exclusion Principle. If it is odd, then it obeys the Exclusion Principle.

Example: Hydrogen has one proton (one proton has three quarks), and one electron (one electron is one lepton); therefore, it does not obey the exclusion theory. An atom of heavy hydrogen (deuteron) has one proton (3 quarks), one neutron (3 quarks), and one electron (1 lepton). Therefore, the number of quarks is odd, and it obeys the Exclusion Principle. It concludes that a deuteron cannot have the same properties as another deuteron atom. On the other hand, properties of the hydrogen atoms can be identical to the properties of another hydrogen atom.

Figure (28): Fermions and bosons forming the atom

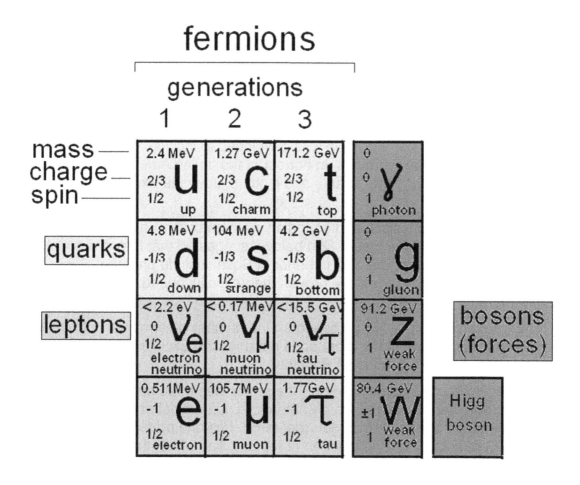

What does the Exclusion Principle mean in practical life? Consider copper and iron wires for conducting electricity. Electrons in the copper wire follow the Exclusion Principle, whereas electrons in the iron wire only slightly follow the Exclusion Principle. Thus, copper wires are better than iron copper in conducting electricity. Laser and photons (light) do not obey the exclusion principle; they are bosons, and have identical properties. This characteristic of light and laser makes them form consistent and solid beams that can travel a long distance.

The nucleus of an atom is a fermion or boson depending on whether the total number of its protons and neutrons is odd or even. Certain atoms can change their behavior if they are subjected to extremely unusual conditions such as very hot or very cold atmospheres.

Bosons are similar to the gravity of our earth. Gravity cannot be seen but it carries a stone, for example, from a higher level to the ground level. Bosons carry the four basic forces in the universe: the electromagnetic, the gravitational, and the strong (gluons which hold the quarks together), and the weak forces that cause the atom to decay (see beta decay above).

The electromagnetic force binds electrons to atomic nuclei (clusters of protons and neutrons) to form atoms.
The gravitational force acts between massive objects. Although it plays no role at the microscopic level (between atoms), it is the dominant force in our everyday life and throughout the universe.
The strong force is responsible for quarks "sticking" together to form protons, neutrons and related particles.
The weak force facilitates the decay of heavy particles into smaller siblings.

19.2 The Standard Model

The most fundamental building block of all matter – the matter that makes up every thing from prokaryotes and eukaryotes to people to galaxies to supernova, and cannot be broken down to any thing smaller is particles known as subatomic particles. For example, the atom is made of protons, neutrons, and electrons. Protons and neutrons are made of particles called quarks, and electrons are made of leptons. Figure (29) shows a helium atom with its subatomic quarks and leptons.

Figure (29): Subatomic quarks of helium atom

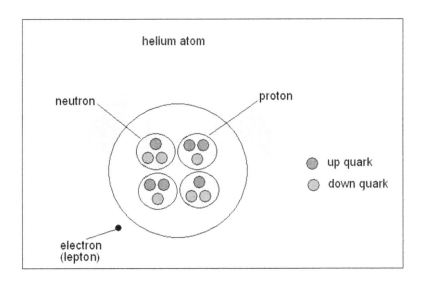

What is a force? Let's take this example. You may have heard of gravity. Gravity is the force that all objects with mass exert upon one another, pulling the objects closer together. It causes a ball thrown into the air to fall to the earth, and the planets to orbit the sun.
The tiny particles that make up matter, such as atoms and subatomic particles,

also exert forces on one another. These forces are not gravity, but are special forces that only these particles use.
There are several kinds of forces that particles can exert on one another. These forces can cause one particle to attract, repel, or even destroy another particle. For example, one kind of subatomic force, known as the strong force, binds quarks together to make protons, neutrons, and other particles

19.3 Particles of Antimatter

Paul Dirac, a British physicist proposed a theory of antiparticles that combine to form antimatter. Antiparticles and particles have the same mass, but their electric charge and colour charge are different. The electric charge and colour charge determine how particles react with each other. Both Fermions and bosons have their own antiparticles.

As protons consist of quarks, antiprotons consist of antiquarks; one antiproton has two up antiquarks and one down antiquark. Similarly, one anti neutron has two down antiquarks and one up antiquark. The antielectron is called a positron, and the muon and the tau have their counterpart's antimuon and antitau. The antiparticles of neutrinos are called antineutrino. Neutrinos and antineutrinos have no electric charge or colour charge. The Antineutrino accompanies the lepton when a proton and neutron decay, and the antineutrino and neutrino balance the output of the decay, Figure (30). Reaction that absorbs neutrino does not absorb antineutrino and vice versa.

Figure (30): Decays of proton, neutron, and fermions

$$u \longrightarrow p + w^- = p + e^- + \bar{\nu}_\mu \qquad p \longrightarrow u + w^+ = u + e^+ + \nu_\mu$$

$$u^- + d = -2/3 - 1/3 = -1 \qquad u + d^- = +2/3 + 1/3 = +1$$
$$w^- = -1 \qquad\qquad\qquad\quad w = +1$$
$$\mu^- + \bar{\nu}_\mu = +1 \qquad\qquad \mu + \nu_\mu = -1$$

Question – can you draw the outcome of an up quark and a down antiquark in terms of electrons and electron neutrinos? Can you determine the outcome of the down quark and up antiquark in terms of positrons and electron antineutrinos?

The standard model has three components: quarks, leptons, and force carriers. The quarks and leptons are categorized into three generations as seen in Figure (28) above. For example, the first generation of quarks is up and down, the second generation is charm and strange, and the third generation is top and bottom. Leptons have the first generation of electron neutrino, the second generation has muon neutrino and muon, and the third generation has tau neutrino and tau. Electrons, like protons and neutrons are stable. Muons and taus are unstable because of their high energy, and are found in decay processes.

Particles made of quarks are called hadrons which are not fundamental, since they consist of quarks. Hadrons can be found in nature as mesons and baryons. Mesons consist of two quarks, and baryons consist of three quarks. Since one boson has two fermions (quarks or leptons), mesons are bosons. The first meson that physicists detected was the pion. Pions exist as an intermediary between protons and neutrons. We shall summarize the four intermediary forces: electromagnetic, gluons, peons, and weak forces in a Feynman diagram, Figure (31).

Figure (31): The four intermediary forces (Feynman diagrams)

Pions are classified as intermediary particles in the nuclei of atoms. They are positive pions, negative pions, and neutral pions as the following equations:

Pion (π^+) = u + d$^+$ = 2/3 +1/3 = 1

Pion (π^-) = u$^-$ + d = -2/3 -1/3 = -1

Pion (π) = u + u$^-$ = 2/3 -2/3 = 0

The average life span of the positive pion is 26 nanosecond (nanosecond = 10^{-6} second) which is the same as the life tome of the negative pion. The average time of the neutral pion is 9 femtosecond (femtosecond = 10^{-15} second). The nucleus of an atom is redrawn to show the above four forces, Figure (32).

Figure (32): Forces in an atom

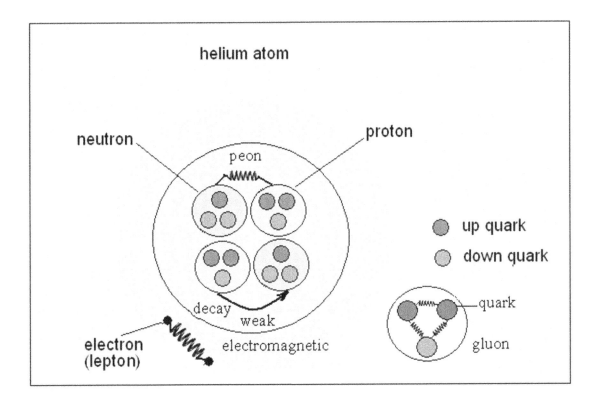

Bosons are the third component of the standard model, and are intermediate force carriers.

The standard model is not a comprehensive theory, since it does not explain why some particles have masses; it needs to be inclusive. Peter Higgs (1929), a British theoretical physicist, introduced his particle "Higg's boson" that could enhance the standard model. Even with Higg's boson, the standard model does not incorporate the gravity, which does not play a significant role in micromatter (such as atoms and subatoms), because gravity is a negligible force on fermions processes. Physicists are now searching for a grand unified theory that includes all forces.

19.4 Grand Unified Theory

The Grand Unified Theory includes gluons (the strong forces or the colour forces), W and Z bosons (the weak forces due to radiation), photons (the electromagnetic forces), and the gravitons (the gravity forces), Figure (33).

Figure (33): The Grand Unified Theory

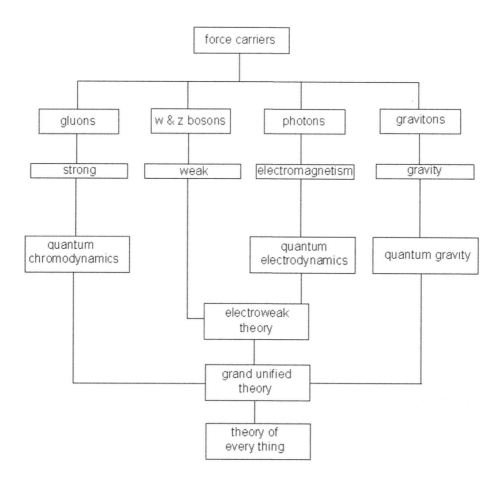

The weak forces (W$^+$, W$^-$, and Z^0) decay to produce other particles. When the weak forces W$^+$ and W$^-$, when interact, change into particles with different charges.

For example, in Beta Decay, one of the down quarks in a neutron changes into an up quark and the neutron releases a W$^-$ boson, (or one of the up quarks in a proton changes into a down quark and the proton releases a W$^+$ boson). This change in quark type converts the neutron (two down quarks and an up quark) to a proton (one down quark and two up quarks). The W boson released by the neutron could then decay into an electron and an electron antineutrino, Figure (34). In Z^0 interactions, a particle changes into a particle with the same electric charge.

Figure (34): Neutron decay to a proton releasing W⁻ which then breaks up into a high-energy electron and an electron antineutrino.

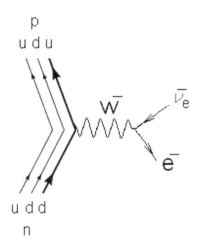

Z bosons are produced when protons and antiprotons collide:

p + p⁻ ⟶ z + other particles

z ⟶ e⁺ + e⁻

z ⟶ μ + μ⁻

Here are other methods of producing Z bosons, Figure (35).

Figure (35): Annihilation of a positron and electron producing Z boson

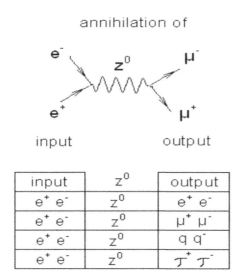

input	z^0	output
$e^+ \ e^-$	z^0	$e^+ \ e^-$
$e^+ \ e^-$	z^0	$\mu^+ \ \mu^-$
$e^+ \ e^-$	z^0	$q \ \bar{q}$
$e^+ \ e^-$	z^0	$\tau^+ \ \tau^-$

19.5 The Higgs Boson

The Higgs Boson is not a force carrier, but scientists believe it gives elementary particles their mass. From the mass of a proton comes the mass of its quarks as well as the energy of the strong force (gluons) holding the quarks together. The quarks, in effect, have no source of mass, which is why the scientists introduced the Higgs boson. Thus quarks obtain their mass by interacting with the Higgs bosons.

Although the Higgs boson has not yet been detected experimentally, scientists are trying to create it through forcing small particles to collide at a high acceleration of such particles. The energy released from the collision could be converted to the Higgs boson. Theoretically, the Higgs boson has a large mass compared to other fundamental particles. Higgs boson can be produced by colliding quarks or leptons together. Figure (36) shows methods of producing Higgs bosons of a high level and of a neutral scalar particle type.

Figure (36): The collision of quarks or leptons to produce Higgs bosons

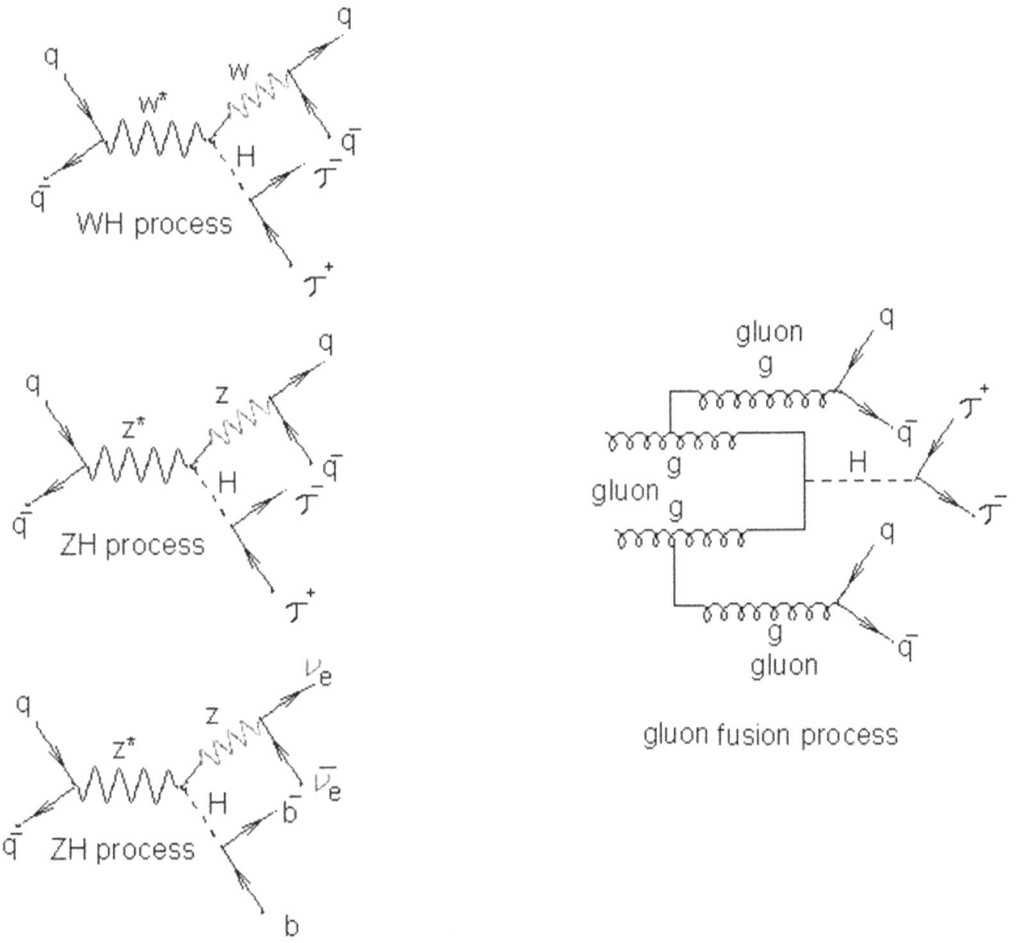

WH process

ZH process

ZH process

gluon fusion process

Despite the remarkable development of the standard model on describing particle physics, the origin of how quarks and leptons have mass is still an open discussion. The answer to this dilemma is the Higgs boson. Scientists are trying to find the Higgs boson at the CERN LHC Large Hadron Collider. The Higgs boson is expected to be produced by gluon-gluon fusion (g-g -> H), or (q-q⁻ -> H) collision (as shown in Figure (19) above). The production of the Higgs boson depends on the Higgs decay mode. For example, if the Higgs is produced below 91.2 GeV and 80.4 GeV, then the Higgs boson will decay to a b-quarks pair. The decay of the Higgs boson depends on the level of GeV of production. Two experiments are close to ruling out a Higgs particle with a mass of 165 GeV/c2 and 175 GeV/c2. At the Tevatron particle collider and the Fermilab collider, scientists increased the GeV in steps (5 GeV). This was done because of the way that the Higgs particle was expected to interact with other subatomic particles, thus the result could be detected in an efficient way, or alternatively, to exclude particles below 114.4 GeV, and to consider those above 160 GeV.

In 2009, the Large Hadron Collider at CERN will begin its hunt for the Higgs boson. The LHC will produce particle collisions with seven times the energy of the Tevatron collider in Batavia, Illinois.

19.6 Higgs Bosons and the Universe

The search for the Higgs boson has been on for ten years, at both CERN's Large Electron Positron Collider (LEP) in Geneva and at Fermilab in Illinois. The Higgs boson (if it is found due to the collision of other particles) will only stay for a small fraction of a second.

Scientists believe that the Higgs boson is responsible for particle mass, the amount of matter in a particle. If the universe was created from nothing (Nothingness theory), then how come the universe has billions of stars and galaxies of colossal masses? According to Higgs' theory, a particle acquires mass through its interaction with the Higgs field, which is believed to pervade all of space and has been compared to molasses which sticks to any particle rolling through it. The Higgs field would be carried by Higgs bosons, just as the electromagnetic field is carried by photons. When any particle hits (or sticks) to the Higgs field, the particle gains mass.

According to the Standard Model, at the beginning of the universe there were six different types of quarks. Top quarks existed only for an instant (life time is 10^{-25} second) before decaying into a bottom quark and a W boson, which means those created at the birth of the universe are extinct. However, at Fermilab's Tevatron, the most powerful collider in the world, collisions between billions of protons and antiprotons yield an occasional top quark. Despite their brief appearances, these top quarks can be detected and characterized by the collider. The bottom quark and the W boson (converting to up and down particles) release energy like a jet, Figure (37).

Figure (37): Proton and antiproton collision

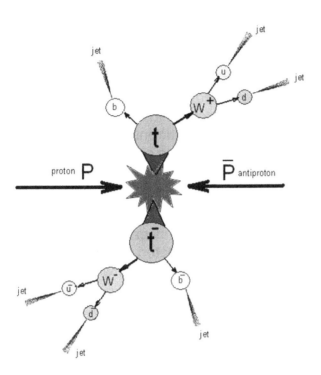

In the Standard Model, the Higgs boson mass is correlated with the top quark mass, (says Madaras from the experimental teams working at the Tevatron's two large detector systems, D-Zero and CD), "so an improved measurement of the top quark mass gives more information about the possible existence of the Higgs boson".

19.7 How the Higgs Field Created the Mass of Everything

The Higgs field is supposed to be responsible for the genesis of inertial mass. When the universe was extremely hot it had zero potential and zero kinetic energy. When the universe started to cool down, the Higgs field assumed some kinetic energy (non zero value), but the potential energy was still of zero value (such an argument has no unique consensus among the physicists). The Higgs field (at zero potential energy and non-zero kinetic energy) continued to influence the whole universe (uniform in the whole universe). Kinetic energy increased when the temperature dropped.

As per Einstein theory $e = mc^2$, the concept of mass–energy equivalence unites the concepts of the conservation of energy and the conservation of mass. This allows kinetic energy or light radiation to be converted to particles which have rest mass, and allows rest mass to be converted to other forms of energy. The total amount of mass/energy remains constant because energy cannot be created or destroyed and, in all of its forms, trapped energy exhibits mass. In relativity and quantum mechanics, mass and energy are two forms of the same thing, and neither one appears without the other.

Now, suppose a fundamental particle (quark or lepton) moves in this uniform Higgs field; the energy of the Higgs field will exert a certain amount of resistance or drag, particularly if the particle changes its velocity; i.e. accelerates. Now the particle has inertial mass due to the gained resistance. A group of particles (say quarks) will be joined together due to the effect of other interaction such as the strong interaction governed by the force of gluons, which glue quarks together into protons and neutrons. Now the mass of protons and neutrons (and atoms) increases. The degree of resistance (drag) of the Higgs field is not the same with all types of quarks and leptons since they are different in shape and type. This creates the difference between the mass of a lepton and that of a quark.

This means that if Higgs field did not exist, then all particles should be massless, like photons. The unification theory stated that when the temperature of the universe was exceedingly high, all differences between all particles disappeared and all forces were one.

19.8 Feynman Diagram

Electromagnetic and weak interaction particle processes were developed by the physicist Richard Feynman. The diagrams he introduced provide a convenient method for the calculation of rates of interaction. In his diagrams, all particles are represented by solid lines, with straight lines representing fermions and wavy lines representing bosons. The Higgs boson is usually represented by a dashed line. Gluons are represented by loops. Particles entering or leaving a Feynman diagram correspond to real particles, while intermediate lines represent virtual particles such as photons and weak forces. Real particles must satisfy the energy-momentum relation $E^2 = p^2c^2 + m^2c^4$, where E is energy, P is momentum, m is mass, and c is the speed of light.

The following rules can be used to represent Feynman diagrams, Figure (38).

Figure (38): Rules of Feynman diagram

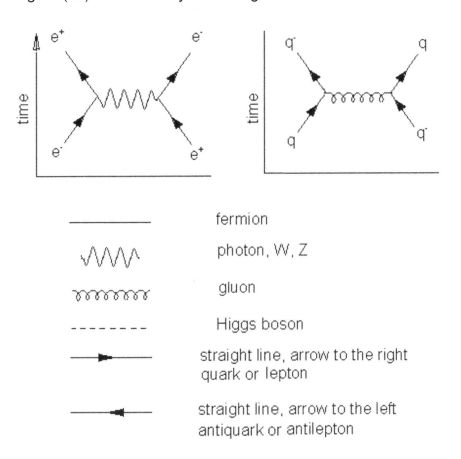

| | fermion |
| photon, W, Z |
| gluon |
| Higgs boson |
| straight line, arrow to the right quark or lepton |
| straight line, arrow to the left antiquark or antilepton |

Examples are shown in Figure (39) below:

Figure (39): Representation of the interaction between electrons, positrons and photons

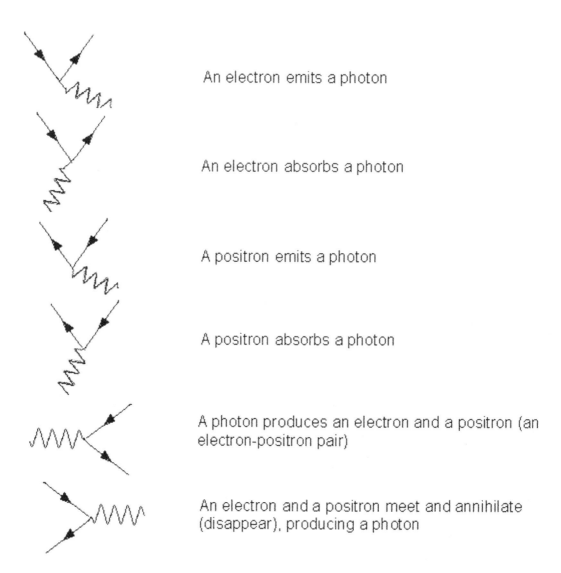

An electron emits a photon

An electron absorbs a photon

A positron emits a photon

A positron absorbs a photon

A photon produces an electron and a positron (an electron-positron pair)

An electron and a positron meet and annihilate (disappear), producing a photon

Similar interactions between fermions (quarks and leptons) are shown in Figure (40).

Figure (40): Representation of the interaction between fermions

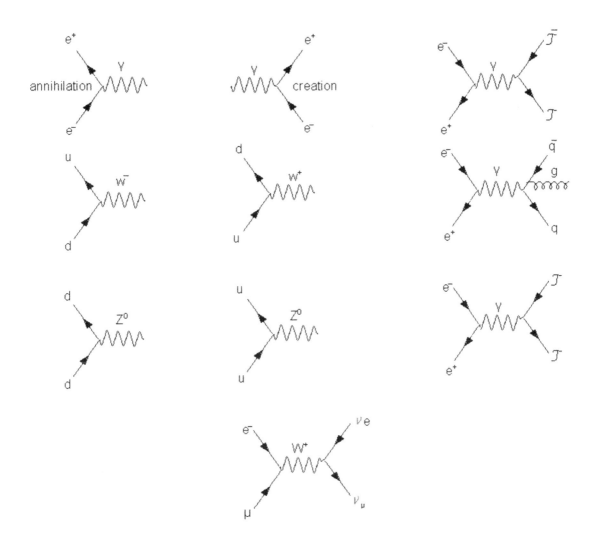

19.9 Supersymmetry

The study of an atom needs two principles: the principle of quantum mechanics (the atom consists of very infinitesimal particles) and the principle of relativity (mass and energy conversion). The marriage between the two is called quantum field theory. The Quantum field theory is the theory behind the anti-matter and the key behind the supersymmetry.

An electron is a point particle, and has no size, yet it has 0.511 MeV. This does not match Einstein's theory, which says that energy has mass. The question is why does an electron have a large amount of energy and is a negligible size (mass). There are two answers to the previous question: either the photon has a mass, or some other particles oppose the movement of the electron. Since the photon does not have a mass, then the other particle that opposes the movement of the electron is the correct answer. It is the positron which is the antimatter of the electron. Similarly, a proton has two up quarks and one down quark of a total energy of 9.6 MeV. A neutron has two down quarks and one up quark of a total energy of 12MeV. The calculated difference is 2.4 MeV, and the actual difference is 1.293 MeV. Therefore, there should be antiquarks to balance the energy in a nucleus.

The Supersymmetric theory stipulates that every type of boson (spin =1) interacts with a type of fermion (spin = 1/2), or the difference between a force and a fermion is ½ spin. The theory gives every particle that transmits a force (a boson) a partner particle (fermion), and vice versa. This means that a fermion cannot coexist with a force. The fermion and the boson are called superpartners, Figure (41). Table (4) shows known particles that transmit forces and their superpartners.

Figure (41): Partners and superpartners

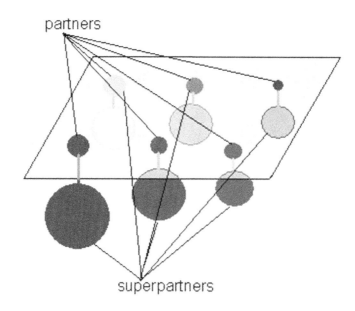

Table (4): Forces and their superpartners

Name	spin	superpartner	spin
graviton	2	gravitino	3/2
photon	1	photino	½
gluon	1	gluino	½
W^+ and	1	Wino$^+$ and	1/2
W^-	1	Wino$^-$	1/2
Z^0	1	Zion	1/2
electron	1/2	selecton	0
muon	1/2	smoun	0
tau	1/2	stau	0
neutrino	1/2	sneutrino	0
quark	1/2	squark	0

Superpartners have not been detected or seen in any previous experiment, but scientists expect to see them in future experiments. Experiments are underway at CERN (we shall discuss this later), and Fermilab to detect supersymmetric partner particles. If that happened, it could lead to the proof of string theory.

19.10 String Theory

The standard model includes particles that move in space without freedom. It has to consider different interactions other than the position and velocity of such particles. Interactions such as mass, electric charge, colour, and spin could give the standard model more freedom. The standard model combines both quantum mechanic and the relativity to include electromagnetic, strong and weak forces. It excludes gravity which was described in the theory of relativity. Therefore, the standard model makes no sense if gravity is neglected. The difficulty in combining the gravity in the mode is due to the fact that gravitons (gravitons mediate gravitational interactions) become infinite, and can not interact with finite particles such as gluons, electrons, muons, quarks, Ws, etc.

In the String Theory all particles, including forces, are replaced by a building block called a string. The shape of the string wiggles like a child jumps on trampoline, or like a string of a guitar vibrates in all directions. The trampoline can be open or closed like a ball, and it is free to vibrate in all directions. The string vibrates in 11 dimensions (one dimension for time, and 10 dimensions for space). Moreover, the string vibrates in different modes, carrying all the four forces, namely, electromagnetic, weak, strong, and graviton.

The String Theory has received so much attention, because it has unified all particles and mediators in one block called the 'Theory of Everything'.

Theorists wanted to simplify the string theory through dividing it into two sub-string theories: the Bosonic String Theory and the Fermionic String Theory. So quarks, for instance, were not included in the Bosonic String Theory, and bosons were not included in the Fermionic String Theory.

19.11 The Large Hadron Collider (LHC)

The LHC accelerator was originally envisioned in the 1980s and approved for construction by the CERN Council in late 1994.
The acronym CERN originally stood, in French, for Conseil European pour la Recherché Nucléaire (European Council for Nuclear Research), which was a provisional council for setting up the laboratory, established by 11 European governments in 1952. Turning this ambitious scientific plan into reality proved to be an immensely complex task. The Large Hadron Collider (LHC) is a gigantic scientific instrument, running along the French-Swiss border. The LHC is a total of 27 kilometers long, and goes100 m underground. It mainly consists of a 27 km ring of superconducting magnets with a number of accelerating structures to boost the energy of the particles along the way.
Inside the accelerator, two beams of particles travel at close to the speed of light with very high energies before colliding with one another. Energies increase through many rounds around the length of the accelerator, and speed up by the accelerators which are made of superconducting electromagnets. The magnets are made of superconducting coils without resistance or loss of energy. Magnets are located in chilling medium frozen to -271°C, a temperature colder than outer space. Thousands of magnets of different shapes and sizes are used to direct the beams around the accelerator. They include 392 quadrupoles magnets of 5-7 meters long to focus the beams, and 1232 dipole magnets of 15 metres long to bend the beams. The particles are so minuscule that the task of making them collide is similar to firing needles from two positions 10 km apart with such precision that they meet halfway. There are six experiments to analyze the myriad of particles produced by the collision in the accelerator: ALICE, ATLAS, CMS, LHCB, TOTEM, and LHCF. The CERN is a particle accelerator to study the smallest known particle – the fundamental building block of all things. It will update our understanding, from the minuscule particle deep within the atom to the immensity of the universe.

The LHC has a circular accelerator of about 27 kilometres, in which two beams of subatomic particles called 'Hadron' – either protons or lead ions (lead has one of the most electronegativities among all elements) will travel in opposite directions, gaining energy with every lap. Team of physicists from around the world will analyze the particles created in the collisions, and compare the results with those just after the Big Bang. Results will help physicists to determine if the standard model can be served as a means of understanding the fundamental law of nature. The most likely explanation may be found in the Higgs field and the Higgs boson, which are undiscovered things that are essential for the standard model to work. Everything we see in the universe forms 4% of the universe and the remaining proportion form the dark matter and the dark energy. The experiment could lead to understanding these two unknown matters. The LHC experiment will be investigating for the difference between matter and antimatter to help answer the question of the reason that matter still exists, while the antimatter has disappeared (hardly any antimatter left after the Big Bang).

There are many questions to be answered from the LHC experiment including:

a) In the very early universe conditions, the temperature was too hot for the gluons to hold the quarks together. Recent science suggests that during the first microseconds after the Big Bang, the universe would have comprised of a very hot dense ocean of quarks and gluons called quark-gluon plasma.

b) We are familiar with only three or four dimensions in space. Can the LHC find other dimensions as the String Theory suggests? Physicists hope that other dimensions will be observed when very high energies are released in the Hadron.

c) Can the LHC find the missing particles which are thought to exist but have never been observed, including Higgs boson, nicknamed the "god particle"? If Higgs boson is observed, then it could answer the question of what causes mass.

d) Will the LHC help our understanding of dark matter (which seems to make up most of the universe) and dark energy (which seems to be accelerating the expansion of the universe)?

There has been speculation that the explosions inside the LHC could create a black hole, which doom-mongers have suggested would swallow the earth. Scientists at the CERN laboratories say that the LHC cannot create black holes, and even if it could, they would be so microscopic that they would immediately disintegrate. Professor Stephen Hawking, the Lucasian professor of mathematics at Cambridge University, said the LHC's power was "feeble" compared with collisions that happen in the universe all the time,

Some pictures of the LHC are shown in Figure (41).

Figure (41): The accelerator LHC

20. Stellar Atmospheres

The stellar atmosphere is the outer region of the volume of a star, existing above the stellar core, the convection zone and the radiation zone. It is divided into several regions of distinct character. The envelope of gas and plasma surrounding a star; consists of about 90% hydrogen atoms and 9% helium atoms. Stellar atmosphere contains some phenomena such as:

20.1 Sun Corona

There is a region around the sun, extending more than one million kilometres from its surface, where the temperature can reach 1.5 million degrees C (the hottest layer of the sun atmosphere). This region, called the Solar Corona, is where the solar wind originates. This bluish white corona has been found to emit X-ray radiation. The corona extends thousands of kilometres into space. The corona can be seen during solar eclipses when the main radiation from the Sun's surface is blocked by the passage of the Moon.

No one can really explain how this corona exists. The temperature in the core of the sun is about 15 million degrees and drops to about 5000 degrees at the surface. The temperature should be even lower farther away from the sun, but the temperature of the corona is measured at more than 1.5 million degrees. This occurrence remained a mystery to astrophysicists. However, some astrophysicists believe that the magnetic field covering the entire surface of the sun is the source of the corona's high temperature. An eclipsed sun with a corona that one can see within the naked eye is shown in Figure (42).

Figure (42): The sun corona during an eclipsed sun

corona around eclipsed

http://www.slac.stanford.edu/
'slac/feature/2006/eclipse/
images/eclipse_10_lr.jpg

20.2 Heliosphere

The heliosphere is a bubble in space produced by the solar wind, and blown
into the interstellar medium, which is composed mainly from hydrogen and
helium. All of the material in the heliosphere originates from the sun itself. The
solar wind streams off of the sun in all directions at speeds of several hundred
km/s. At the orbit of Pluto the speed reaches supersonic level, and then slows
down as it meets the gases in the interstellar medium. First, it passes the so
called "shock boundary", after which it slows down to a subsonic speed. It then
slows down to form a comet-like tail behind the sun. This subsonic flow region
is called the helio-sheath. The outer surface of the helio-sheath, where the
heliosphere meets the interstellar medium, is called the heliopause, which is
where the interstellar medium and solar wind pressures balance each other.
The point where the solar wind slows down is the termination shock, Figure
(43).

Figure (43): Heliosphere with its boundaries (not to scale)

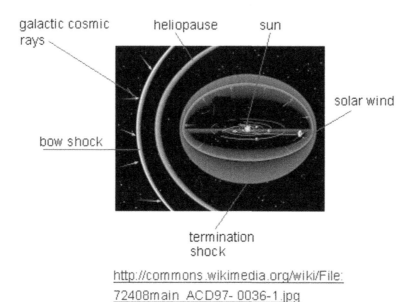

galactic cosmic rays

heliopause

sun

solar wind

bow shock

termination shock

http://commons.wikimedia.org/wiki/File: 72408main_ACD97-0036-1.jpg

20.3 Solar Wind

Stream of protons and electrons flow from the sun's corona outward at speeds between 300 and 1000 km per second. The streams come from holes in the sun's corona, and push the gas of the comets' tails away from the sun, causing geomagnetic disturbances on the surface of the earth. As the stream of atomic particles (protons and electrons) approach earth, they cause gases in the earth's upper atmosphere to heat up and expand, then cool down and contract. This changes the upper atmosphere's density and electromagnetism. This could reduce the natural shielding that envelops our solar system, particularly our earth. Solar wind inflates a protective bubble, or heliosphere, around the solar system. Other phenomena include geomagnetic storms which would influence things such as environment, biological reaction, telecommunication and power grid lines. Moreover, the solar wind interacts with every planet in our solar system, and also defines the boundary between our solar system and interstellar space. The solar cycle from maximal to minimal activity affects the pressure and magnetic field of the earth. Solar wind makes the transition from a supersonic flow at an altitude of about 4 solar radii from the photosphere, to a sonic flow at an altitude of about 1.5 solar radii. The flow of the sonic wind now appears to be much lower, perhaps only 1 solar radii above the photosphere, suggesting that some additional interaction accelerates the solar wind away from the sun. This makes the total mass loss each year about $(2–3) \times 10^{-14}$ solar mass or 6.7 billion tonnes per hour. This is equivalent to losing a mass equal to the mass of the earth every 150 million years, http://en.wikipedia.org/wiki/Solar_wind. However, only about 0.01% of the Sun's total mass has been lost through the solar wind. Other stars have much stronger stellar winds that result in significantly higher rate of mass loss. NASA scientists claim that the sun seems to be losing power, A study released by NASA reports that the solar wind has hit a 50-year low. The average pressure of the solar wind has dropped almost 20%! This has no consequence (as of yet) to people on Earth. Even though this trend may be unusual in the 40 years we've been measuring the solar wind, it's likely just a blip in the 4.6 billion years the sun has existed.

21. High Energy Astrophysics (Nuclear Astrophysics)

The stars are powered by nuclear fusion processes. The most important two nuclear processes occurring in nature are the p-p fusion and the CNO cycle (p stands for proton, and CNO stand for carbon, nitrogen, and oxygen). Both of the two processes contribute to hydrogen burning. The rates at which the two processes react depend on the temperature of the star and its surrounding atmosphere. The slowest reaction in the p-p chain (the weak interaction) is as follows:

$$^1H + {}^1H \longrightarrow {}^2H + e^+ + \nu_e$$

The fusion of two protons results in one alpha particle, one positron, one neutrino, and energy. The proton-proton chain reaction occurs in small stars such as our sun. In heavier stars, the CNO cycle occurs.

In the CNO cycle (the electromagnetic radiation), carbon, nitrogen and oxygen are exchangeable as follow:

$$^1H + {}^{14}N \longrightarrow {}^{15}O + \gamma$$

In the CNO cycle, the reaction can be completed in much shorter time scale than the p-p chain, because the p-p reaction is limited by a weak interaction.

The p-p chain in the sun is represented by:

$$p + p \longrightarrow {}^2H + e^+ + \nu_e \qquad 1.44\,\text{MeV}$$

$$p + \bar{e} + p \longrightarrow {}^2H + \nu_e$$

$$^2H + p \longrightarrow {}^3He + \gamma \qquad 5.49\,\text{MeV}$$

$$^3He + {}^3He \longrightarrow \alpha + 2p$$

where α is a helium atom of two protons and two neutrons

The Above equations can be represented by Figure (44).

Figure (44): Reactions of p – p chain

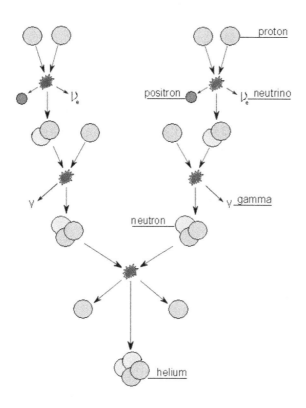

The p-p chain reaction is one of several fusion reactions by which stars convert hydrogen to helium, helium to lithium, and lithium to beryllium. The p-p chain reaction occurs in stars the size of the sun or smaller. There are four branches of p-p chains: pp1, pp2, pp3, and pp4. Branch pp1 takes place with a frequency of 86%, pp2 with 14%, and pp3 with 11%. Branch pp4 is extremely rare. The three branches of pp1, pp2, and pp3 are described below:

pp1 branch: ^3He + ^3He $\longrightarrow$ ^4He + ^1He + ^1He +12.86 MeV

^3He + ^3He $\longrightarrow$ ^4He + 2p + 12.86 MeV

pp2 branch: ^3He + ^4He $\longrightarrow$ ^7Be + γ

^7Be + $\bar{e}$ $\longrightarrow$ ^7li + ν_e

^7li + 1H $\longrightarrow$ ^4He + ^4He

pp3 branch: ^3He + ^4He $\longrightarrow$ ^7Be + γ

^7Be + ^1H $\longrightarrow$ ^8B + γ

^8B $\longrightarrow$ ^8Be + e^+ + ν_e

^8Be $\longrightarrow$ ^4He + ^4He

Figure (45) shows the flow of reaction of the pp1, pp2 and pp3 chains.

Figure (45): The flow reaction of the pp1, pp2 and pp3 chains

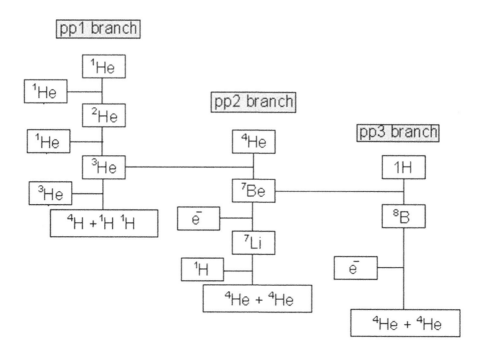

Stars spend their lives burning the hydrogen existing within their cores. In all three pp branches, the star exists in hydrodynamic stability.

In the CNO cycle, the electromagnetic radiation occurs to produce Gamma rays which exchange the carbon to nitrogen, and the nitrogen to oxygen. The CNO cycle operates on a much shorter timescale than the p-p chains. Proton (hydrogen) can also interact with the CNO cycle as follows:

$$^{12}C + {}^{1}H \longrightarrow {}^{13}N + \gamma$$

$$^{13}N \longrightarrow {}^{13}C + e^+ + \gamma$$

$$^{13}C + {}^{1}H \longrightarrow {}^{14}N + \gamma$$

$$^{14}N + {}^{1}H \longrightarrow {}^{15}O + \gamma$$

$$^{15}O \longrightarrow {}^{15}N + e^+ + \nu_e$$

$$^{15}N + {}^{1}H \longrightarrow {}^{12}C + {}^{4}He$$

The flow reaction is shown in Figure (46).

Figure (46): The flow reaction of the CNO cycle

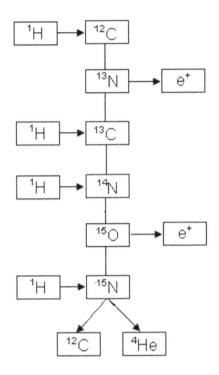

A secondary branch of the CNO cycle could affect the abundance of ^{16}O in the stars, starting at ^{15}N. The reactions are:

$$^{15}N + {}^{1}H \longrightarrow {}^{16}O + \gamma$$

$$^{16}O + {}^{1}H \longrightarrow {}^{17}F + \gamma$$

$$^{17}F \longrightarrow {}^{17}O + e^{+} + \nu_{e}$$

$$^{17}O + {}^{1}H \longrightarrow {}^{14}N + {}^{4}He$$

The flow reaction of the above reaction is shown in Figure (47).

Figure (47): The reaction of the secondary branch of CNO cycle

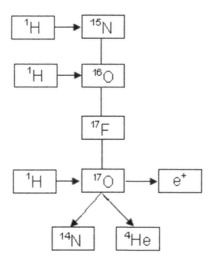

http://www.chemistrydaily.com/chemistry/Triple-alpha_process

22. Galaxies in the Universe

The existence of our galaxy, the Milky Way, was only proven in the 20th century, along with the existence of "external" galaxies, and soon after, the expansion of the universe. Modern astronomy has also discovered many strange objects such as quasars, pulsars, blasars, and radio galaxies. These observations have been used to develop physical theories which describe some of these objects in terms of equally strange objects, such as black holes and neutron stars. Physical cosmology made a huge development during the 20th century, with the theory of the Big Bang greatly corroborated by the evidence provided by astronomy and physics, such as the cosmic microwave radiation, Gamma and X-Ray radiation, and Hubble's principle.

It is theorized that earth was formed as part of the birth of the sun. The sun was composed of hydrogen and helium produced in the Big Bang, as well as denser elements ejected by supernovas. Then, as one theory suggests, about 4.5 billion years ago a nearby star was destroyed in a supernova and the explosion sent huge impulses through the solar system and galaxy system, causing it to gain angular momentum. As the rotating cloud flattened out, some of the gas and dust clustered together due to gravity (which eventually becomes the planets). Because the initial angular momentum needed to be conserved, the clustered mass started rotating faster. The current rotation period of the Earth is the result of this initial rotation and other factors such as friction and a giant sudden impact.

Although the science of astronomy has made great steps in understanding the nature of the universe and its contents, there remain some important unanswered questions. A deeper understanding of the formation of stars and planets is needed.

22.1 Composition of the Universe

Scientists believe that the universe is mainly composed of dark energy and dark matter, Figure (48).Ordinary matter is about 4% which causes perturbation

Figure (48): Composition of the universe

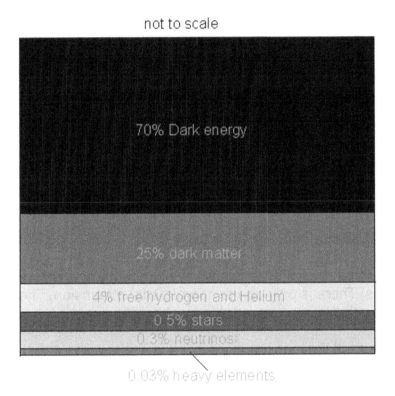

22.2 Elementary Particles of the Universe

The universe is constructed from matter and forces. Matter is comprised of six leptons and six quarks. An atom has protons and neutrons, both are composed of quarks and leptons. The matter and forces interact with each other as shown in Figure (49). The Higgs boson is believed to give mass on all particles. The gauge boson of gravity (graviton) is deleted from the figure, because it is still disputed in the model of quantum cosmology.

Figure (49): Interaction of forces and matter of the universe

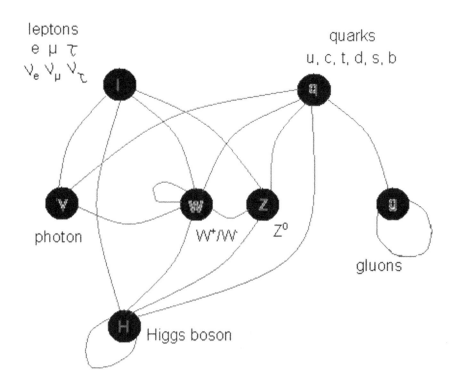

22.3 Special Relativity and Space-time

The universe has at least three spatial dimensions. It has recently been proven to have eleven dimensions. There is only one temporal (time) dimension. The spatial and temporal separation is interconvertable by changing one's displacement.
For example, consider the spatial dimension as
$L = \text{SQRT} (X^2 + y^2)$,
$L = \text{SQRT} (m^2 + n^2)$, and the displacement angle is α, Figure (50).

In one spatial dimension, the transition matrix can be written as:

$$\Phi (1,1) = \begin{array}{|c|c|} \hline 1 & 1 \\ \hline 0 & \alpha \\ \hline \end{array}$$

The connection matrix can be rearranged to:

$$c (1,1) = e^{-j\alpha} \begin{array}{|c|c|} \hline 1 & 0 \\ \hline 0 & 1 \\ \hline \end{array}$$

Where $e^{-j\alpha} = \cos \alpha - j \sin \alpha$

The transition matrix for two spatial dimensions and one temporal dimension can be written as:

$$\Phi (2,1) = \begin{bmatrix} 1 & 0 & 0 \\ 0 & \alpha & 0 \\ 0 & 0 & \alpha \end{bmatrix}$$

The corresponding connection matrix is:

$$c (2,1) = e^{-j\alpha} \begin{bmatrix} 1 & 0 & 0 \\ 0 & 1 & 0 \\ 0 & 0 & 1 \end{bmatrix}$$

Above matrix can be rearranged as:

$$c (2,1) = \begin{bmatrix} \begin{matrix} \cos \alpha & \sin \alpha \\ -\sin \alpha & \cos \alpha \end{matrix} & 0 & 0 \\ 0 & \begin{matrix} \cos \alpha & \sin \alpha \\ -\sin \alpha & \cos \alpha \end{matrix} & 0 \\ 0 & 0 & \begin{matrix} \cos \alpha & \sin \alpha \\ -\sin \alpha & \cos \alpha \end{matrix} \end{bmatrix}$$

So, the space-time interval between two spatial galaxies (or two events) can be calculated if the distance and the rotation displacement are known.

Figure (50): Space-time configuration

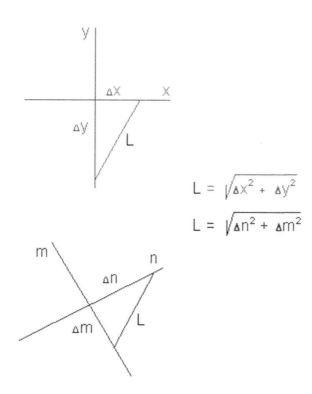

special relativity

$$L = \sqrt{\Delta x^2 + \Delta y^2}$$

$$L = \sqrt{\Delta n^2 + \Delta m^2}$$

22.4 Real-time

Real time is measured from any reference frame external to a black hole. The reference frame can have any particle or energy, and can be related to the black hole using an appropriate conversion matrix. The distance between the reference frame and the black hole can be adjusted if the light speed between the two positions is measured. If the space-time is bent at a point, the conversion matrix can be used at that point, and then referred to the conversion matrix between the reference frame and the black hole. For example, a star is located at point (x, y, z, t1, t2) where x, y, and z are location of the star form the black hole, t1 is the time required to travel from the star to the point (a) where the light is bent, and t2 is the time from the point to the black hole. The correlation can use the following formula:

93

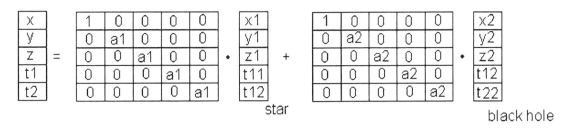

star

black hole

Absolute real-time (the unbend) has the fastest time-frame. Multiple time-frames could be used when the light is bent. An other time-frame could also be used to relate one star to another.

22.5 Shwarzchild Radius

Karl Shwartzchild calculated the necessary density of matter which would be required to boost the escape velocity from that matter to the speed of light. The Shwartzchild radius is the distance between the centre of the black hole and the outer boundary where the escape velocity equals the speed of light, Figure (51). The density of mass inside the black hole decreases to a limit sufficient enough to raise the escape velocity to the speed of light limit at this radius.

Figure (51): Shwartzchild radius

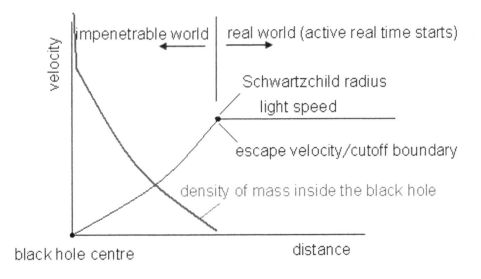

22.6 The Comedy-Recycling (C-R) Theory

The C-R theory predicts that there will be another inside boundary, and an inner Schwarzschild radius. Between these two Schwarzschild boundaries, the inner and outer radii will be a filled shell, a dense volume, or a zone, which the

C-R theory has termed the Neutral-Zone, Figure (52). Anything trapped between the inner and outer Schwarzschild radii, (in the Neutral-Zone), is suspected to be impervious, and unaffected by any and all time.

The quantum theory proposed that there was a minimum energy orbital for an electron. At that orbit, the electron could not radiate away any further. The amount of energy in one of its orbiting zone can be represented as the Shwarzchild neutral zone. On the contrary, the classical theory (false assumption) postulates that the constantly moving electron would continually radiate away all of its energy until the electron collapsed entirely into the proton (proton can be represented as

The C-R theory suggests that the minimum gravitational energy for any particle occurs in the neutral zone or before the active real time starts.

Figure (52): Shwartzchild boundaries

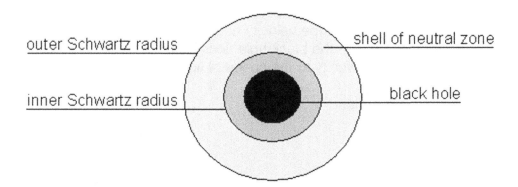

Let us discuss the effect of gravity based on the C-R theory. When a matter changes its speed or path, kinetic energy will be released. This suggests that the matter gains some gravitational forces due to the released energy. The released energy would have been converted to heat or work. The following equation expresses the conversion:

$$E = mc^2 = m_{after} \, c^2_{\ after} + \text{energy released}$$

Therefore, either the quantity of mass or the speed of light will decrease to balance the energy conservation. In small distances, no one can notice the difference in mass or speed as the changes are minuscule. The changes in mass and speed would be sizeable if the matter travels to either the outer edge of the universe or the Great Attractor.

Above equation can be rewritten as:

$$E = mc^2 = m_{after} \, c^2_{\ after} \times \text{the change in real time}$$

In other words, 1 ton of rocks (matter) at the Great Attractor are worth less energy than the same mass transported to our earth. The difference between the two energies is the same gravitational energy required to lift the matter from the Great Attractor to the earth. Thus, the gravity is proportional to the real time difference between two locations.

22.7 Galaxy Rotation Curve

The rotation curve of the Orion Galaxy can be represented by a graph, Figure (1), which plots the velocity of the orbit of the sun or the gas in the galaxy on the Y-axis, against the distance from the centre of the galaxy on the X-axis. Stars revolve around the centre of galaxies at a constant speed over a certain distances from the centre of the galaxy. The observed speed is much faster than would be expected within a free in Newtonian space, Figure (53). The speed of the galaxy around the centre does not match scientific analyses and calculations. This is true for visible objects, but what about dark objects that penetrate the orbit? Does it mean that electromagnetic wave that carry photons of light have an effect on the speed? Or does a black hole change its gravity during its penetration? Such problems are to be solved and answered by scientists.

Figure (53): Faster observed speed of galaxies than expected

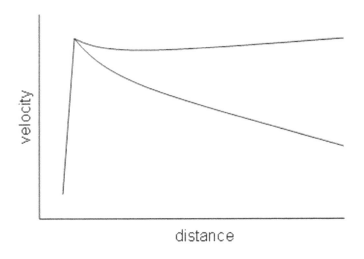

23. Doppler Effect in Sound, and Red Shift and Blue Shift in Light

When a police car releases its siren, you will hear a different pitch as the car zooms towards you. As the car approaches you, the waves of sound are compressed together, and you hear a different higher pitch. When the car passes by, the sound waves expand, and you hear a lower pitch of sound, Figure (54). This apparent change in the pitch (or frequency) of sound is called Doppler shift.

Figure (54): Doppler Effect

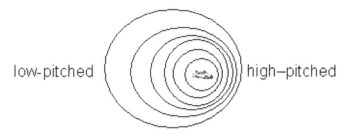

low-pitched   high–pitched

Light from stars and galaxies are shifted in much the same way. A star approaching towards you has its light waves compressed together, and you see a higher frequency of light than normal. It means that the visible frequency has been changed towards the blue colour. It is then said that the star is blue shifted. Similarly, as the star moves away, the light wave broadens, and you see lower frequency of light spectrum. This is called a red shift, Figure (55).

Figure (55): Red shift and Blue shift

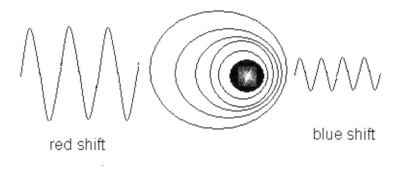

red shift   blue shift

On earth, we see the light from stars and galaxies moving away from us. As the universe expands, the redder they become.

The frequency of the light depends on the speed of the star moving away from us. In order to change 1% in the frequency of light, a star has to move 1,864 miles per second. For a blue light lamp to look red, it would have to move away from us at 0.75 of the speed of light.

Astronomers have noticed that galaxies and stars farther away from us are more red shifted than closer ones. This concludes that the farther ones are moving away from us in a faster pace.

24. Stars

A star is ball of hydrogen and helium with enough mass that it can sustain nuclear fusion at its core. Our sun is a star.

When a supernova explodes or a galaxy collides, stars are created due to the collapse of a cloud of gas (mainly hydrogen and helium).

The collapsed cloud heats up from the gravitational force, and over the course of 100.000 years, it gets hotter and hotter becoming a baby star (T Tauri star). The baby star shines with just the gravitational energy, but without nuclear fusion. After 100 million years of collapse, temperatures and pressures become sufficient for nuclear fusion. When the nuclear fusion starts, the star completes it formation.

The least massive star is the red dwarf star and is about 75 times the mass of Jupiter. A red dwarf star could live 10 trillion years. The largest super giant star, on the other hand, has a very short life. For example, the Eta Carinae star has about 150 times the mass of the sun and is emitting more than1 million times as much energy as the sun, but has a very short time to live (in the range of a few million years). When super giant stars die, they burst into powerful supernovae.

24.1 Active Galaxies

An active galaxy is a galaxy which has a small core with enormous amount of energy seen in the centre. This core may be highly variable and very bright compared to the rest of the galaxy. The intense radiation produced by hot gas in the core is an accretion disk around a black hole. Active galaxies have black holes in the centers. The mass of the black hole must be hundreds of millions to several billion solar masses in order to keep the gas spiraling in and heating up. The accretion disk is a few trillion kilometers across (a few light months across) but most of the intense radiation is produced within a couple hundred billion kilometers from the black hole. The energy emitted from normal galaxies is equal to the sum of the emission from each of the stars found in the galaxy. For the active galaxy there is a great deal more emitted energy than there should be. This is because the energy radiated by the black hole(s) in the centre.

The dramatics are the high-energy exploding away from some supermassive black holes. These jets move at nearly the speed of light in tight beams that blast out of the galaxy and travel hundreds of thousands of light years.

The central black hole is assumed to be surrounded by a thick donut-shaped cloud of gas and dust, Figure (56).

Figure (56): Magnetic field and jet of high speed particles emitting from an active galaxy

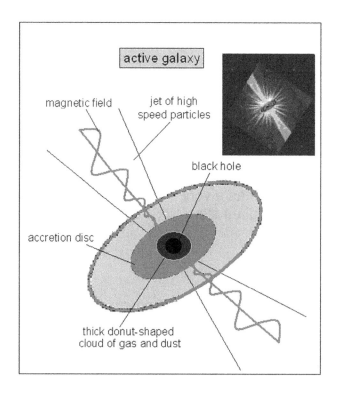

Duccio Macchetto, an ESA astronomer, Head of the Science Policies Division, STScI quoted "Hubble provided strong evidence that all galaxies contain black holes millions or billions of times heavier than our sun. This has quite dramatically changed our view of galaxies. I am convinced that over the next ten years the Hubble will find that black holes play a much more important role in the formation and evolution of galaxies than we believe today. Who knows, it may even influence our picture of the whole structure of the Universe...?"

So, based on Hubble's findings, all galaxies have black holes probably located in their centres. Active galaxies and quasars must have the black holes of a supermassive mass.

24.2 Quasars

Quasars are farther away from earth than any other known object in the universe. Because they are so far away from us, it takes billions of years for the light they give off to reach earth. The light stays the same; it just has to travel a long time to get to us. When we look at a quasar, it is like we are looking back in time. The light we see today is what the quasar looked like billions of years ago. Some scientists think that when they study quasars they are studying the beginning of the universe.

Quasars are the centres of active galaxies and give off more energy than 100 normal galaxies combined. Quasars give off radio waves, X-rays, gamma-rays, ultraviolet rays, and visible light.They can be seen in different views. A black hole with energetic jets beaming out can be seen from two sides. When the beam is directed towards us we see the bright lighthouse of a quasar. When the orientation of the system is different we observe it as an active galaxy or a radio galaxy. This is called the unified model. This 'unified model' has gained considerable support through a number of Hubble observational programs. The simplistic early ideas have, however, been replaced by a more complex view of this phenomenon – a view that will continue to evolve in the years to come.

Many astronomers believe that quasars are the most distant objects yet detected in the universe. Quasars give off more energy than 100 normal galaxies combined. They can be a trillion times brighter than the Sun's energy. Quasars are believed to produce their energy from massive black holes in the center of the galaxies in which the quasars are located. Because quasars are so bright, they obscure the light from all the other stars in the same galaxy. In one second, a typical quasar releases enough energy to satisfy the electrical energy needs of earth for the next billion years. Energy from quasars takes billions of years to reach the Earth. For this reason, the study of quasars can provide astronomers with information about the early stages of the universe.

24.3 Seyfert Galaxies

Seyfert Galaxies are a class of galaxies with nuclei that produce spectral line emissions from a highly ionized gas, named after Carl Keenan Seyfert, the astronomer who first identified the class in 1943, [C. K. Seyfert (1943). "Nuclear Emission in Spiral Nebulae". Astrophysical Journal 97: 28–40. doi: 10.1086/144488]. The centres of Seyfert galaxies form a subclass of active galactic nuclei (AGN), and are thought to contain supermassive black holes with masses between 10^7 and 10^8 solar masses. The tremendous brightness of Seyferts can change over periods of just days to months and some galaxies are suspected of harboring massive black holes at their cores.
As an example, a Seyfert galaxie of type NGC 7742 has spiral arms, ringed by blue-tinted star forming a centre of 3,000 light-years across, and it is about 72 million light-years away from the constellation Peasus. It is harboring massive black holes at their cores.

24.4 Blazars

A **blazar** (a combination of a **bl**ack hole and a qu**asar**) is a very compact quasar associated with a presumed supermassive black hole at the centre of an active, giant elliptical galaxy. Blazars are among the most violent phenomena in the universe.

A blazar is believed to be an AGN that has one of its relativistic jets pointed toward the Earth so that what we observe is primarily emissions from the jet region. They are similar to quasars, but are not observed to be as luminous.

The visible and gamma-ray emission from blazars is variable on timescales from minutes to days.

The relationship between the luminosity emitted in the rest frame of the jet and the luminosity observed from Earth depends on the characteristics of the jet and the observed angle. Also, the luminosity from a jet depends on the magnetic fields within the jet and the shocks arising from the interaction between the gravity and the blazar's wind. The luminosity from a jet observed from the earth is shown in Figure (67).

Figure (57): Luminosity of a blazar from the earth

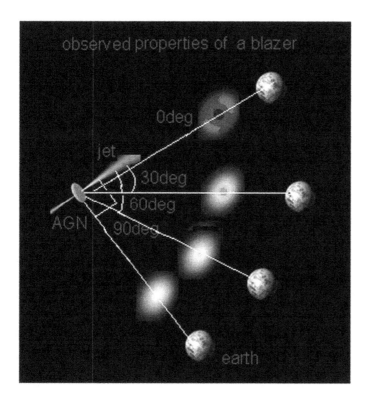

24.5 White Dwarf

A white dwarf is a star whose nuclear fuel has been exhausted.

At the end of its nuclear fission stage, the star expels most of its outer material, creating a planetary nebula. Only the hot core of the star remains. The core becomes a very hot (> 100,000K) young white dwarf, which cools down over the course of the next billion years or so.

A typical white dwarf is half as massive as the Sun, yet only slightly bigger than the Earth. This makes white dwarfs one of the densest forms of matter known, surpassed only by other compact stars such as neuron stars, black holes and hypoteticallt quark stars, [*Exotic Phases of Matter in Compact Stars*, Fredrik Sandin, licentiate thesis, Luleå University of Technology, May 8, 2005].

With a surface gravity of 100,000 times that of the earth, the atmosphere of a white dwarf is very strange. The heavier atoms in its atmosphere sink and the lighter ones remain at the surface. Some white dwarfs have almost pure hydrogen or helium atmospheres, the lightest of elements. The white dwarf is shown in Figure (58).

Figure (58): Picture of a white dwarf

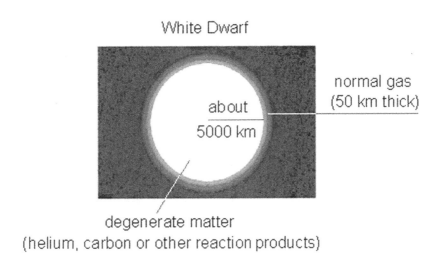

White Dwarf

about 5000 km

normal gas (50 km thick)

degenerate matter
(helium, carbon or other reaction products)

24.6 Supernova

A supernova is one of the most explosive events known in the universe. Conventional theories ascribe the creation of supernova (plural supernovae) due to the explosion which occurs at the end of a star's life time, when its sore energy is worn out, and the core is collapsed, releasing a huge amount of energy. The star is usually denser and heavier than our sun. The released energy causes a blast wave that ejects the star's surrounding envelope into interstellar space. The blasted envelope becomes a rotating neutron star that can be observed many years later as a radio pulsar. Since the star exhausted its last nuclear hydrogen available for fusion into helium, the only remaining nuclear fuel would be helium and heavier elements, up to iron and lead. In a fraction of a second, the supernova would expand more energy than an entire galaxy of stars. The entire outer portion (the envelope) of the parent star's mass would be expelled at a tremendous velocity.

The C-R theory suggests that an increase in neutrino is released at the moment the external envelope of the star expelles. The C-R theory predicts that very sharp burst of extremely energetic, positively charged particles (protons) are released and accumulated in the neutral zone. High energy cosmic rays are caused from those protons in the neutral zone. The C-R predicts that any fusion reaction in a supernova occurs as a side product, not as the root cause of the nova-supernova phenomenon.

24.7 Black Hole

A black hole is a region of space time from which nothing can escape, not even light. It is impossible to see a black hole directly because it attracts the light and no light can escape from it; it becomes black. Black holes are created from the remnants of large stars after they burn their fuel. When a large star burns, it explodes into a supernova. The remnant that is left collapses down to an extremely dense object known as a neutron star. The gravity of the neutron star pulls its particles and objects to the centre, creating a black hole. The supernova occurs in our galaxies about every 300 years. The identified number of neutron stars is 500. This means that there should be some black holes in our neighboring galaxies.

24.8 Black Hole Bigger than Previously Thought

In the past, astronomers were not able to add dark matter into their low power computers to calculate traces of the orbits of stars and galaxies. Now, astronomers Karl Gebhardt, from University of Texas and Jens Thomas, of the Max Planck Institute for Extraterrestrial Physics in Munich, Germany, have added dark matter to a simulation of the galaxy M87, a colossal galaxy about 55 million light years away. Gebhardt and Thomas found massive black holes which are two to three times more massive than astronomers thought. When they added dark matter to the model, they surprisingly found that the central black hole was 6.4 billion times the mass of our sun, Figure (59). Previously, It was thought that the black hole was about 2 to 3 billion times the sun.

Figure (59): Black hole bigger than previously thought

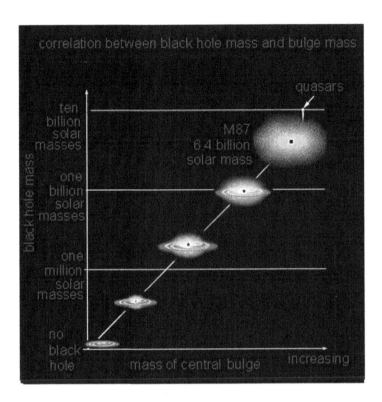

25. Acceleron and neutrino

Two of the biggest breakthroughs recently are the accelerons and neutrinos. These two subatomic particles are linked to the so called dark energy. Dark energy was insignificant in the early understanding of the universe. Neutrinos are created by the trillions during the nuclear fusion of stars such as our sun. Dark energy results as the universe tries to pull neutrinos apart, producing an energy which energizes the expansion of the universe, said Ann Nelson, a UW physics professor. Neutrinos pass through all matters, including people, but they have no electrical charges, and therefore have no interaction with the materials they pass through.

Accelerons have not yet been detected by sophisticated detectors, and they have little interaction with matter. However, accelerons exhibit forces that can influence neutrinos which can be detected by a variety of neutrino detectors already available around the world.

The force between neutrinos and accelerons can be measured to calculate the rate of expansion of the universe. However, the measurement is difficult to obtain because this requires the observation of very distant object. Another problem in the measurement is that the spinning and the mass of neutrinos can change according to the environment through which they are passing.

Physicists have pursued evidence that could tell whether the universe will continue to expand indefinitely or come to an abrupt halt and collapse on itself in a so-called "Big Crunch." While the new theory doesn't prescribe a "Big Crunch," Nelson said, it does mean that at some point the expansion will stop progressing at faster rate.

"In our theory, eventually the neutrinos would get too far apart and become too massive to be influenced by the effect of dark energy any more, so the acceleration of the expansion would have to stop," Nelson said. "The universe could continue to expand, but at an ever-decreasing rate."

26. Critical Density

Critical density of the universe determines its geometry. If the density of the universe is less than the critical density, then the universe is curved like the surface of a saddle. The universe looks like a sphere if the critical density is less than its density. The universe is flat if the critical density equals its density, Figure (60).

Figure (60): Critical density and geometry of the universe

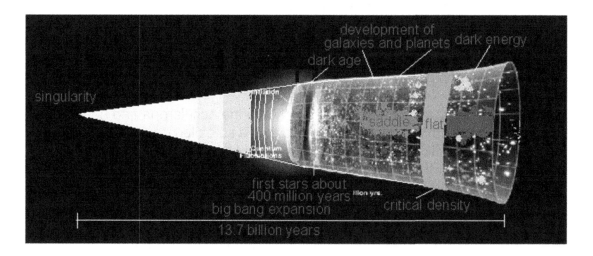

The fate of the universe depends on the critical density. If the density of the universe is greater than the critical density, then the universe will reach the so called Big Freeze or Big Crunch, and the universe will eventually collapse. If the critical density is greater than the density of the universe, then the universe will expand.

27. Average Distance between Galaxies

Micheal Rowan-Robinson, Professor of Astrophysics at Imperial College London explained the Hubble's measurements of the distances to several galaxies in the following equation:

H = v/D where H is the Hubble constant, v is the recession velocity and D the distance, Figure (61).

Figure (61): Hubble constant curve

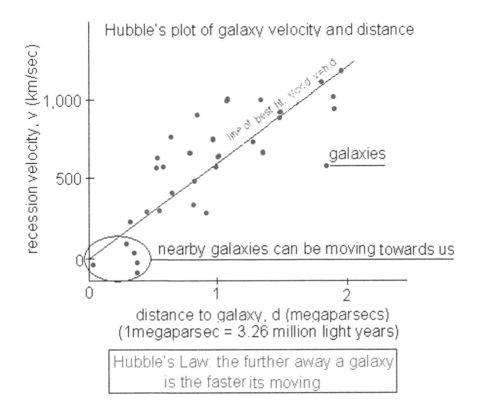

Suppose v/D = H then

a (acceleration) = dv/dt = d(Hd)/dt = HdD/dt + DdH/dt where dH/dt =0

Therefore, a = HdD/dt = Hv = HHr = H^2r

The cosmological acceleration was calculated to be $6 \times 10^{-10} m/s^2$.

The above analysis neglects the time between two distant galaxies, where the light may be bent. During this time, velocity v is quite likely to change. So Hubble constant should consider the time rather than the distance (v/t instead of v/D). Since velocity is likely to change, then expansion of the universe depends on two factors: distance and acceleration. If we consider the term v/r which equals to 1/t, then we refer to the age of the galaxies (universe).

Moreover, if Hubble constant (H) equals v/D, then we talk classic physics, but the universe is quantum physics. So, the term v/D is rejected when combined to come up with a quantum gravity theory.

The universe is expanding at an accelerating rate (cosmological acceleration), according to startling new evidence suggesting that a mysterious antigravity force permeates "empty" space and is counteracting the pull of gravity on a cosmic scale. Scientists suggested that such an antigravity force must be a mix of ordinary matter and some kind of unseen dark matter of an exotic nature.

28. Unsolved Scientific Puzzles

Here are some of the most puzzling anomalies of modern science, those intractable and defiant problems that can not conform to the theories:

28.1 Weak Nuclear Force

Radiation could emit one type of ray called "beta decay" which is the emission of an electron from a neutron in the nucleus of the atom, converting it into a proton. Such an emission could convert one chemical element to another, but so feebly that its origin was named 'the weak nuclear force'. As well as in radioactivity, the emmission plays a vital role in the burning of the sun, and other stars. As energy (temperature) increases, the weak force gets stronger. In the extreme temperatures during the birth of the universe, we now realize that electromagnetism and the weak force was one and the same thing. As this fireball cooled down, it eventually reached a temperature where the weak interaction froze. Beta radioactivity and other low energy weak force effects are only the fossil remains of what happened in the beginning of the creation of the universe. Albert Einstein spent much of his life unsuccessfully trying to weld gravitation and electromagnetism. Abdus Salam and Steven Weinberg, working independently in the mid 1960s, came up with a pioneering solution. These powerful intuitive ideas needed to be examined with experiment. Also, the theory could not yet be cast in a form capable of providing precise, unique predictions. By 1971, the theoretical recipe had been completed but not verified, and it was up to experimenters to make the next steps. The theory, now usually called the Electroweak Theory (a name adopted by Salam), predicted the existence of heavy particles to communicate the weak force. It also indicated that they would have two types, now called W (which is the communicator when the particles involve reciprocal electrical charges) and Z (when no charge exchange takes place). This leads to the recognition of quantum mechanics of the known two energies 'enthalpy' and 'entropy' in the universe, which is similar to Newtonian term 'kinetic' and 'potential energy' on earth. This is later called W and Z bosons. At the birth of the universe, the force W was so infinite that it could destroy the whole universe, and convert back to gases and dust. Then, as per the Big Bang theory, it returns back to a different universe.

The accelerator, estimated to cost between $5 billion and $10 billion, could provide answers to questions physicists have had for decades. Thousands of scientists from around the world are collaborating on the project at the European Organization for Nuclear Research, or CERN. The accelerator will explain the interactions of matter with three of the four fundamental forces of nature: electromagnetism, the strong nuclear force (which binds the parts of a nucleus together) and the weak nuclear force (which allows for the radioactive decay of particles). Its collection of particles consists of bosons — which mediate these forces — and fermions, which combine to make up the matter. The leading scientist behind this huge project is the physicist Nima Arkani Hamed who thinks that the universe has at least 11 dimensions.

28.2 Theory of de Sitter-Like Universe

The puzzle that has no explanation of black holes (which rotate and or carry electric charges) undergoes a second order phase transition, in which specific heat changes from negative to positive in an unsymmetrical pattern. This was analyzed by the de Sitter phase theory. Black holes get hot if they loose energy, see Pavón and Landsberg (1988).

According to Hawking (1975) the entropy (S) and temperature (T) of the black hole are:

$$S = \pi.\, rh^2 = 4.\pi.M^2$$

$$T = k/2\pi = 1/8\pi.M$$

Where rh = radius of the event horizon, k is the surface gravity and M is the mass of the black hole. Then follows:

$$\delta S/\delta T = -64\,\pi\,M^3 < 0$$

If the Black hole possesses angular momentum α and /or electric charge Q, then

$$\alpha \rightarrow Q = \delta S/\delta T = > 0 \ (Davis\ 1978).$$

These transitions of negative to positive values of $\delta S/\delta T$ occur through infinite discontinuity of the second order thermodynamic phase transition. Science can not explain the physical phenomenon of such a transition. If the transition occurred rapidly, this would destroy the black hole, and therefore, all black holes would vanish. There are millions of black holes now existing in the universe.

28.3 God Does Not Play Dice in the Universe as Claimed by Einstein

Newton, in his laws used deterministic mechanics in his interpretation of the macrophysics analysis, (which is similar to an athlete running around a circle). Newton can "determine" the position and momentum of the athlete at any subsequent time, as long as some other object doesn't interfere with it. Other physicists did not agree with Newton, if the athlete run around a circle with a speed equal to the speed of light, i.e. Newton's Laws cannot be applied to microphysics.

Werner Heisenberg of the so-called Copenhagen School claimed that the behaviour of the constituents of matter (atom) is not deterministic, but it is indeterministic. He devised that from the Quantum Mechanics theory.

Einstein disagreed with this conclusion based on his definition of causal and predictive determinism. He agreed on causal determinism in macrophysics, but he doesn't agree that causal determinism in microphysics is false since the concept of causal determinism is embedded within the predictive determinism. Einstein was completely correct if we consider the matter of logic, and also physics. If we consider that energy comes in multiples of little packets called "quanta" meaning that such packets have causal determinism. In logic formulas:

cause + angular momentum = causal determinism,
causal determinism + angular momentum = predictive determinism

This means that the movement of the moon around the earth has a cause at a certain point and certain time, i.e.; there is a cause of controlling the sun and stars and also the universe. That is why he said "God does not play dice in the universe". It means that God control the universe.

God does not play dice with the universe; He plays an ineffable game of his own devising, which might be compared, from the perspective of any of the other players, to being involved in an obscure and complex version of poker in a pitch dark room, with blank cards, for infinite stakes, with a dealer who won't tell you the rules, and who smiles all the time. By Terry Pratchett, "Good Omens"

28.4 The Oh-My-God Particles

Some cosmic rays possess energies that are too large for science to solve their origin and structure. Cosmic rays with even higher energies were observed on the evening of October 15, 1991, by the University of Utah's Fly's Eye Cosmic Ray Detector. Astrophysicists were shocked at its energy, which was estimated to be about 3×10^{20} eV (electron volt) which is equivalent to a brick falling on your toe, and such energy emerged from one proton (one atom from hydrogen contains one proton). That energy is enough to light a 40 watt light bulb for more than a second. The energy travels at a speed of 0.9999999999999999999999995 of the speed of light or about 29999.97 km per second (the speed of light equals about 300,000 km per second), or lag the light by 30 meters per second.

The source of these ultra high energies is interrelated with extragalactic super-massive black holes at the centre of nearby galaxies, such as the Andromeda Galaxy, called the active galactic nuclei. The theory behind the origin of these energies is uncertain. Other possible sources could be radio rays from powerful radio galaxies, hypernovae, Gamma-ray bursts, or intergalactic shocks created during the epoch of the galaxy creation. The perceived time to travel to our sun is 1.5×10^{-6} milliseconds and to our galaxy's centre is 3.2 seconds. Astrophysicists call these particles of high energies "Oh-My-God particles". Can you calculate how many particles needed to destroy our Earth using the formula:

$$M1 \vec{U1} + M2 \vec{U2} = M1 \vec{V1} + M2 \vec{V2}$$

Is this formula valid when two objects travel at the Newtonian principle (the earth) and the other object travel at the Einsteinium Principle (the particles)? Can science find a solution to this dilemma?

28.5 Is the Time Constant since the Creation of the Universe?

There was no time before the creation of the universe. A decade ago, scientists discovered that fundamental constants of physical equations might not be so constant after all. The speed of light is constant and has two components: the distance and the time. Light that has traveled across the universe between distant stars tells us those laws might have been different in the past.

28.6 Galaxies Are Racing Away From Us Far Faster Than Scientific Theories Predict (by NASA).

Could the reason be that objects placed closer to the centre of the vortex (centre of the galaxies) orbit at a greater speed than objects further out from the center, in accordance with Kepler's Laws? Or, could the depression (hollow) in the centre of the universe be a relative absence of matter producing an effect of a characteristic of gravity, i.e. the gravity in the centre is smaller than the gravity in the exterior, therefore, a larger gravity attempts to nullify a smaller gravity. Thus, a larger volume of space (universe) will be created in the exterior area. The nullification of gravity is inversely proportional to the distance, and that is why the galaxies are leaving us faster than previously predicted. Recently, the Hubble Deep Field has supported such a phenomenon.

28.7 Puzzle of the Rotation Curve of the Solar Planets

Because the strength of the gravitational force and the angular momentum of the sun decrease with distance from the sun, it accelerates the inner planets more than the outer planets. This is shown in Figure (62). However, when we look to the planets and their speed, we see something very different. In the inner galaxy, the rotation speed rises with an increasing radius.
Another peculiar thing is that massive stars such as black holes do not follow the law of spin versus gravity and weight. Thus a black hole that is at the center of a galaxy with the weight of a million stars spins a million times faster than one with the weight of one star.

Figure (62): Calculated and actual orbital speed

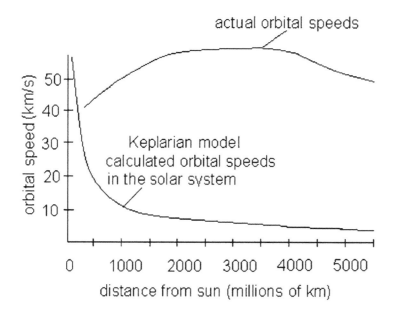

28.8 Tetraneutrons (Four Neutrons Are Bound Together)

The particle accelerator in France detected six particles that should not exist. A group of them are called tetraneutrons, meaning four neutrons that are bound together in a way that confronts the laws of physics. Francisco Miguel Marquès and colleagues at the accelerator will do the experiment again to confirm the certainty of the tetraneutrons. If they succeed, this may change the whole theories of quantum physics and alter our understanding of the fermions and the forces of nuclear physics. According to the Pauli exclusion principle, not even two protons or neutrons can be held together.

28.9 Dark Matters

If the speed of the outer stars in spiral galaxies is higher than the speed of inner stars, then spiral galaxies do not wind up. This is true if we calculate the speed of stars, considering that the rotation speed rises with increasing radius. In reality, the inner stars are faster in their spinning speed than the outer stars. Scientists contributed the high speed of the inner stars to the fact that there should be huge masses outside the spiral galaxies. They call them "dark matters". This could be true because If the speed of the outer stars in spiral galaxies is higher than the inner stars, then each spiral galaxy does not end up, resulting in the destruction of all spiral galaxies because all of them would fall apart.

28.10 Dark Energy

In 1998, astronomers noticed that the universe is expanding at ever faster speeds. It's a phenomenon is still not explained. Before this discovery, scientists thought the universe's expansion was slowing down after the Big Bang. Katherine Freese of the University of Michigan, Ann Arbor suggested that some property of empty space is responsible - cosmologists call it dark energy. But all explanations have fallen short. It's also possible that Einstein's theory of general relativity may need to be fine-tuned when applied to the very largest scales of the universe. "The topic is still wide open for research ," Freese says.

28.11 Flouting the laws of physics

In the 1970s NASA launched two space probes that have caused no end of headaches. About 10 years into the missions of Pioneer 10 and 11, the mission head admitted that they had drifted off course. In every year of travel, the probes veer 8000 miles further away from their intended trajectory. It is not much when you consider that they cover 219 million miles a year; the drift is around 10 billion times weaker than the Earth's pull on your feet. Nonetheless, it is there, and decades of analysis have failed to find a straightforward reason for it (The Times , April 11, 1974). Does this mean that the weak nuclear force and the electromagnetic force were not unified? Science tells us that they are unified.

29. What the Three Religions Said About the Creation of the Universe

The three main religions believe that humanity, life, the earth, and the universe are the creation of a supernatural being (God). As science developed from the 18th century onwards, various views developed which aimed to reconcile science with the sacred books.

29.1 The Jewish Faith

The Sabbath Brought Stability to the World:

Jewish people believe that God created the world during the original six days, and rested on the Seventh. They think that God refrained from His creative activities on Sabbath, and did not introduce anything new into the world. But did God perhaps "create" something on the Sabbath? The Talmud indicates (BT Chagigah 12) that yes, something new certainly was introduced into the fabric of the world with the advent of the Sabbath.

It was the element of permanence. "The world was unstable and shaky," say the rabbis, "until the arrival of the Sabbath... then the earth was firmly anchored into place." Why? What is it about the Sabbath that brought "stability" to the world? Before the Sabbath, the whole of creation was a shaky and insecure thing. It is as if the permanence of creation was debatable, uncertain, an open question hanging in the balance until the arrival of the seventh day. It almost seemed as if there was some doubt as to whether or not this would be a sure thing. The earth hung suspended in the universe, lacking a sense of cohesion, quivering and heaving with the possibility that perhaps all is only temporary.

Indeed, something about the Sabbath had the capacity to bring the world its sense of permanence, and lock it into place... but just what is it?
The powerful answer is both beautiful in its simplicity and staggering in its depth: The Holy Sabbath is the soul of the world; it is the soul of creation itself.

This is the mystery of the words "And on the seventh day, He refrained (from work) and 'Vayinafash' - He rested..."

The Creator stopped His work, on account of this ' Vayinafash', "and He rested", according to its simple meaning, but actually a form of the word 'nefesh' means soul. For the secret contained within these words is that when the Holy One stopped the process of creation, in doing so, "vayinafash" - the nefesh, the life-force was brought down into each level of creation and became fixed there within in a permanent fashion. Before the Sabbath came, the world literally stood by like a body without a soul, and every aspect of creation was devoid of the inner essence of life. The holy Sabbath day became the soul of all creation, and through it, existence became whole.

The Sabbath Brings the Soul.

Again, it is the secret of the first Sabbath. We have now seen that it was necessary for the first Sabbath to arrive upon the world to fill God's creation with the soul (the inner essence for life). By establishing the eighth day of life as the day in which to perform the circumcision, then if a minimum of eight days pass over the child, this will include one Sabbath. Thus, the child will be prepared to enter into the holy "brit", the covenant of circumcision. For he will have that same inner strength, that soul-power which only the Sabbath can bring. In the words of the rabbis, he will be a "baal nefesh", literally, one with a soul. Just as the Sabbath brought the world its soul, every child is filled with that same life-force and quality of permanence by the arrival of the first Sabbath in his life.

And so we return to the words with which this verse begins - "And God completed."

Previously we had asked, if God created something new on the seventh day because the verse would seem to imply that He completed His activity on the seventh day.

The Permanence of Creation

We have explained that the day of the Sabbath itself brought the aspect of conclusion to creation. This was the completion which the verse refers to. When God "concluded His activity on the Sabbath," it was not that something was missing from creation which had yet to be provided, but rather all had been created and was not lacking in completion, it was lacking in firmness and stability. It was this that came about through the Sabbath.

That Sabbath confirmed the permanence of existence. But during those first days of creation, prior to the arrival of the Sabbath, are we to understand that everything in the universe simply hung on in standby status? If so, then what power drove the universe?

God Himself revealed the answer to this question in the language of the Ten Commandments, in the words of the commandment which relates to Sabbath (Exodus 20). But if we examine the words carefully, not as many people erroneously read, "For God created the world in six days...", but, the verse clearly reads "For six days. God created the heavens and the earth..."

The World Exists from Sabbath to Sabbath

The Sabbath's unique quality and power is that it recharges and renews the spiritual energy of the world. The other weekdays literally derive their nourishment from it. This applies to the entire structure of creation. Without this system of replenishment, the world would not survive, but after six days it would immediately implode, returning to the chaotic state of "emptiness and void". As the Torah states: "For six days God created the world". After this, without the life-giving energy of the holy Shabbat, God would have to create the world again

Every new week that passes over us is actually sustained by and receives its very life-force from the holy Shabbat. All of creation is given the ability to function for yet another week by the influx of the divine influence which it receives on this day.

Do not think that this is in any way a contradiction or limitation to that which we have learned earlier, that the power which drives the world is its collective desire to come closer to the light of God. For without the Sabbath, the world would lack the perception of God's presence in the creation which is necessary to fan those flames of desire and longing. The two concepts are actually part of the same process.

29.2 The Christian Faith

Everyone agrees that it has been at least thousands of years since the time of creation, yet the Bible declares that God rested on the seventh day after His six days of creation (Gen. 2:2-3). According to the book of Hebrews, God is still in His Sabbath rest from creation (4:3-5); hence, the seventh day has been at least six thousand years long, even on the shortest of all the chronologies of humankind.

- The Third "Day" Is Longer Than Twenty-Four Hours.
- The Sixth "Day" Is Longer Than Twenty-Four Hours

In Mark 10:6, Jesus quotes Genesis 1:27: "From the beginning of creation God 'made them male and female.'" Many young-earth creationists have latched onto this verse, interpreting it in a novel way that provides evidence for their position of a 6,000 to 10,000 year old earth. However, careful study of this passage reveals the traditional understanding of Jesus' words as correct and the passage does not support a recent creation as per John Battle, Professor of the New Testament.

Sun Created After the Day

The Bible says in chapter 1, verses 3-5, of Genesis that the phenomenon of day and night was created on the first day of the creation of the Universe by God. The light circulating in the universe is the result of a complex reaction in the stars; these stars were created according to the Bible (Genesis chapter 1 verse 14 to 19) on the fourth day. It is illogical to mention that the result is the light (the phenomenon of day and night) was created on the first day of creation, when the cause or source of the light was created three days later. Moreover the existence of evening and morning as elements of a single day is only conceivable after the creation of the earth and its rotation around the sun.

The phenomenon of day and night was created on the first day of creation of the Universe by God). These stars were created according to the Bible (Genesis chapter 1, verse 14 to 19), on the fourth day.

According to the Bible, (Genesis, chapter 1, verses 9 to 13) the earth was created on the third day, and according to Verses 14 to 19, the sun and the moon were created on the fourth day.

According to the Bible, Book of Genesis, chapter 1, verses 11-13, vegetation was created on the third day along with seed-bearing grasses, plants and trees; and further on as per verses 14-19.

29.3 The Muslim Faith

"God rules the cosmic affair from the heavens to the earth. Then this affair travels, to Him (i.e. through the whole universe) in one day, where the measure is one thousand years of your reckoning"(Quran 32:5)

Creator of the heavens and the earth from nothingness, [He has only to say when He wills a thing: "Be," and it is] (Al-Baqarah 2:117) and, [That is how God creates what He wills, when He decrees a thing, He says "Be," and it is] (Aal `Imran 3:47).

"He created the heavens and the earth In true (proportions): He makes the Night Overlap the Day, and the Day Overlap the Night." [Al-Qur'aan 39:5]

"And the earth, moreover, Hath He made egg shaped." [Al-Qur'aan 79:30]

In the creation of the heavens and the earth, and the alternation of night and day, there are Signs for people with intelligence. (Qur'an, 3: 190).

"Do not the Unbelievers see that the heavens and the earth were joined together (as one unit of Creation), before We clove them asunder?"[Al-Qu'ran 21:30]

Moreover, He Comprehended in His design the sky, and it had been (as) smoke: He said to it and to the earth:'

"Come ye together, willingly or unwillingly.' They said: 'We do come (together), in willing obedience.'"[Al-Qur'an 41:11].

"It is God who created the seven heavens and of the earth the same number, the Command descending down through all of them, so that you might know that God has power over all things and that God encompasses all things in His knowledge." (Qur'an, 65: 12)

Among the proofs given in the Qur'an there is a very detailed explanation of the different features of the universe, how it was made and how the planets and stars were formed. Allah says that, "To Him is due the origin of space and the Earth." (6:101)

The Qur'an does not give a single, unified essay on how the universe began. Instead, keeping with the Qur'anic method of teaching, different aspects of creation are mentioned in different places in order to give authority to the particular lesson being taught. (See 30:58)

For example, in Surah at Tariq, (86) Allah begins by mentioning the brightest star that appears in the sky at night. Then He describes this star and uses it as a metaphor for how every human has an angel watching over them. Do you see how Allah uses physical aspects of nature to illustrate spiritual principles?

Allah begins by stating that the universe and planet Earth took six "days" to create. (7:54). Now it must be remembered that in Arabic the word Youm can mean a day as we know it, or it can mean any stage or period of time. As Allah points out, a day to him can be a thousand years, fifty thousand years or more.(Qur'an).

The creation of planets and the Earth took place in the last two periods of time. As Allah states in the Qur'an, "Declare, 'Do you disbelieve in the One Who created the Earth in two stages? Do you make others equal to Him? He is the Lord of all the worlds.'" (41:9)

Space was filled with matter, anti-matter and gases which eventually combined into larger particles. These bits of matter eventually grew into asteroids, planets, stars and moons. Each object of inter-stellar space conformed to a set of physical laws which governed the trajectory of their orbits so a regular pattern of rotation could be seen. (21:33, 29:61)

Stars ignited in a fury of radioactive fusion and gave off light and heat which brought warmth to those planets near them. (86:3) Small moons were captured in the orbit of larger planets and came to have a regular orbit around them, often reflecting light from the sun. (54:1-2)Finally, the planets themselves developed and formed in a variety of ways, with fantastic geologic formations and movements, both above and below the surface. (The planet Earth, in particular, cooled near its outer layers, forming a thin crust made up of plates that moved and grated against each other. (15:19) This allowed the Earth's surface to constantly erase the damage caused by occasional asteroid impacts. The colliding of the plates also had the side effect of raising tall mountains and exposing the geological history of the planet.

30. Other Faiths and Creation of the Universe

Since the beginning of time, humans have questioned the existence of the universe and many different theories concerning the physical world have been popularized. One such theory is the creation theory. It asserts that the universe and humans, as well as the rest of the natural world, were created by one or more supernatural beings or gods. For instance, Genesis, a book of the Bible, is one creation theory, telling the story of God creating the universe and the first humans in seven days. The Quran says that the universe was created in six days. However, there are other theories about the creation of life by a supernatural being or God.

There are different theories about the creation derived from Biblical and Quranic verses, and all of them oppose scientific forms of dating the universe and the earth, and oppose evolutionary concepts. We shall see in the following sections what different faiths theorize and believe on the creation of the life and the universe.

30.1 Mesopotamian and Babylonian Mythologies

The earliest mention of the city of Babylon can be found in a tablet (characters and figures were imprinted on a wet clay tablet with a stylus often made of reed) from the reign of Sargon of Akkad, dating back to the 23rd century BC.

Mesopotamians and Babylonians (present-day is Iraq) were the first civilization and were probably founded about a century after the collapse of Sumer *circa.* 2004 BC.

Mesopotamian mythology is the collective name given to Sumerian, Akkadian, Assyrian, and Babylonian mythologies from parts of the Fertile Crescent, the land between the Tigris and Euphrates rivers in Iraq.

The Sumerians envisioned the universe as a closed dome surrounded by a primordial saltwater sea. Underneath the terrestrial earth, which formed the base of the dome, existed an underworld and a freshwater ocean called the Apsu. The god of the dome-shaped firmament was named An; the earth was named Ki. The underground world was first believed to be an extension of Ki, but later developed into the concept of Kigal. The primordial saltwater sea was named Nammu, which became known as Tiamat during and after the Sumerian Renaissance, [The Firmament and the WaterAbobe. Westminster Theological Journal 53 (1991), 232-233].

Sumerians believed that the gods originally created humans as servants for themselves but freed them when they became too much to handle.

The primordial union of An and Ki produced Enlil (Lord of the Wind, En = Lord), who became leader of the Sumerian panthion. After the other gods banished Enlil from Dilmum (the "home of the gods") for raping Ninlil (the Lady of the Air), Ninlil had a child: Nanna, god of the moon. Nanna and Ningal (the Great Lady) gave birth to Inanan (Goddess of sexual love, fertility, and warfare) and to Utu, god of the sun, [Enlil and Ninlil. Electronic Text Corpus of Sumerian Literature].

So, the Babylonian story about the creation of life started in late 12th century BCE. The sequence of creation is as follows:

The universe was created after a God won the battle with a Goddess.

The earth was then created and enveloped in darkness. It was called "Chaos".

Firmament was (sky) created and perceived as a rigid dome

Dry land was created.

Sun, moon, and stars were created.

Men and women are created.

God rests and celebrates.

The gods of the Babylonians became the ancient Israelites' god, [http://www.religioustolerance.org/com_geba.htm].

30.2 Ancient Greece

Greek astronomy is understood to include the ancient Greek, Hellenistic, Greco-Roman, and Late Antiquity eras. Greek astronomy is also known as Hellenistic astronomy, while the pre-Hellenistic phase is known as Classical Greek astronomy.

The development of astronomy by the Hellenistic astronomers is considered by historians to be a major phase in the history of astronomy in Western culture. It was influenced by Babylonian astronomy; in turn, it influenced Islamic, Indian, and Western European astronomy.

Hellenistic astronomers believed their gods lived in the skies and had different names. They named those gods in nature names such as god of wind, god of water, god of sun, etc. They also named the constellation stars with names as they were seen, for example, Taurus, Libra, Cancer, Gemini, etc.

The ancient Greeks believed that in the beginning of the creation, the universe was Chaos, an amorphous and void, and surrounded an unending stream of water ruled by the god Oceanus. The universe was the domain of a goddess named Eurynome which was far-ruling and wandering.

Eurynome controlled the universe and when she wanted she could make order out of the universe (the Chaos). Eurynome coupled with a huge powerful snake (or the North Wind) and gave birth to Eros, god of Love (Protagonus). Eurynome separated the sky from the sea by dancing on the waves of Oceanus. In this manner, she created great lands upon which she might wander, a veritable universe, populating it with exotic creatures such as nymphs, Furies, and Charites as well as with countless beasts and monsters.

Also born out of Chaos were Gaia, called Earth, or Mother Earth, and Uranus, the embodiment of the Sky and the Heavens, as well as Tartarus, god of the sunless and terrible region beneath Gaia, the Earth. The earth was flat.

They believed that gods have powers that are lost to us in the physical body. Many seek to activate these powers now.

After the Hellenistic period, Greeks believed in the geocentric model or the Ptolemaic model. Ptolemy suggested that the earth is the centre of the universe and other objects orbit around it. Belief in this system was common in ancient Greece and was followed in the Hellenistic period. The Ptolemaic model was also embraced by Aristotle. Both ancient Greek and ancient Chinese philosophers assumed that the sun, moon, stars and visible planets revolve around the earth each day. The stars circle around the pole and those stars closer to the equator rise and set each day and circle back to their rising point. The earth is solid and stable; it is not moving and is at rest. In this period, they believe that the earth is a spherical shape.

The Ptolemaic model was gradually replaced the Copernicus, Galileo and Kepler models.

30.3 The Baha'i Faith

Baha'is believes that God has revealed Himself to humanity through a series of divine Messengers, whose teachings guide and educate us and provide the basis for the advancement of human society. These Messengers have included Abraham, Krishna, Zoroaster, Moses, Buddha, Jesus, and Muhammad. Their religions come from the same source and are in essence successive chapters of one religion from God.

Baha'u'llah, the latest of these Messengers, brought new spiritual and social teachings for our time. His essential message is of unity. He taught the oneness of God, the oneness of the human family, and the oneness of religion.

Baha'u'llah said, "The earth is but one country and mankind its citizens," and that, as foretold in all the sacred scriptures of the past, now is the time for humanity to live in unity.

For Baha'is, the concepts of Heaven and Hell are allegories for nearness and remoteness from God. When we die, the condition of our souls determines our experience of the afterlife. Heaven and Hell are not physical places, but spiritual realities.

Baha'is do not have a scientific or theoretical explanation or interpretation about the creation of the universe. However, they believe that only one God exists and He created the whole world.

30.4 Buddhism

In Buddha teachings, The Universe (and all that is in it) is ordered by impartial, unchanging laws. These laws have been operating throughout all time into the infinite past and will continue to operate into the infinite future. There never was a first beginning, and there never will be a final end. The Buddha further said that there are at least a billion other world-sun systems like our own, and as these grow old and die out new solar systems evolve and come into being. Yet, unlike the laws of physics and chemistry, the course of events is not a blind matter of chance. Buddhism regards the Universe as a harmoniously functioning whole with a unity behind its diversity. Man was created by the laws of nature; the world was not created for man.

Ancient Buddhists imagined the universe as essentially flat, with Mount Meru (Mount Meru is a sacred mountain in Buddhist, Hindu and Jain mythology) at the centre of all things. Surrounding this universe was a vast expanse of water, and surrounding the water was a vast expanse of wind.

This universe was made of thirty-one planes of existence, stacked in layers, and three realms, or *dhatus*. The three realms were Ārūpyadhātu, the formless realm; Rūpadhātu, the realm of form; and Kāmadhātu, the realm of desire. Each of these was further divided into multiple worlds that were the homes of many sorts of beings. This cosmos was thought to be one of a succession of universes coming into and going out of existence through infinite time.

Our world was thought to be a wedge-shaped island continent in a vast sea south of Mount Meru, called Jambudvipa, in the realm of Kāmadhātu. The earth, then, was thought to be flat and surrounded by ocean.

30.5 Confucianism

The history of Confucianism and Taoism goes as far back as the time of Fu Hsi, (pronounced as Foo She) (c. 3322 BC), who was both a king and a great sage.

Confucians believe that *Tai Chi* is the Ultimate, an integrated energy of *Yin* and *Yang,* which is evolved from *Wu Chi* (void energy) and can be transformed into various forms. The ultimate source of all energy and knowledge is called *Tao,* which is a continuum without boundaries in time and space, infinite, formless, and luminous (I-Ching). In Confucian philosophy, the system of Yin and Yang was conceived as a way of explaining the universe. It is a purely relativist system; any one thing is either Yin or Yang in relation to some other object or phenomena, and all things can be described only in relation to each other. The Yin and Yang are the negative and positive principles of universal force and are pictorially represented by the symbol of Tai Chi.

Recent Confucian literature mentioned that it is not difficult to prove that Confucianism is not a man-made philosophy at its origin. It did embrace the idea of one immortal God, from whom its teachings originated and who is believed to govern the universe. "Heaven" is a manifestation of that God, and as such sometimes He Himself is referred to as Heaven. Confucianism considers true knowledge to consist of understanding the attributes of God and adopting them in one's own conduct. This brings man closer to eternal truth and serves as a source of knowledge for his benefit.

30.6 Druze

The Druze are a break-away sect from orthodox Islam that appeared in the 9th Century CE. They are regarded by the mainstream Muslim scholars as Kafirs or unbelievers. The Druze are a religious community found primarily in Syria, Lebanon, Israel, and Jordan.

To Druze, God has been believed to be the Creator of the Universe. It has been believed that He created the heaven and the earth when He wished to create them, and that He is the ruler of this universe, yet He is higher and far beyond all Being.

Another sect of Druze is that God is not only beyond the universe, nor is He only higher than it; God is Existence as such, and accordingly He is the only

Existent; nothing outside Him exists. He is the Whole. No limitation can be attributed to Him. He is unlimited.

They believe in the transmigration of the soul: that at death, one's soul is instantaneously reincarnated (in time and space); it is reborn into another life. Through successive reincarnations, the soul eventually unites with the Cosmic Mind "al- aaqal al kulli or "the whole mind" The Cosmic Mind is considered as "God's will" and from this cosmic mind the universe came into being.

They are firmly monotheistic, believing in a single God. God has no partner or son; he is not part of a Trinity. God created the universe from nothing, and is omnipotent and omniscient.

30.7 Ancient Egyptian Religion

The ancient Egyptian Religion is a religious universe stretching over a period of time of about 4000 years, from before 3000 BCE until the 6th century CE in Ancient Egypt. This corresponds to the cultures centered on the river Nile in today's Egypt and northern Sudan.

The Egyptians conceived of the earth as a disk, with the flat plains of Egypt as the center and the mountainous foreign lands as the rim surrounding and supporting the disk. Below were the deep waters of the underworld, and above was the plain of the sky. Several systems of cosmic deities arose to explain this natural phenomenon. Some attributed the creation of the world to the ram god Khnum, who styled the universe on his potter's wheel. Others said that creation was a spiritual and not a physical act, and that the divine thought of Ptah (Intellectual god) shaped the universe.

Before creation there was only sea. Re, the sun-god, came out of an egg or a flower, and from him other deities came. One deity became the earth, another the sky, a third the god of the dead etc. In certain regions, other gods were honored for the creation of cosmos, like Ptah was in Memphis, the sun in Heliopolis and Hermopolis, and Khnum on the island of Elephantine.

In one dynasty, Egyptians believed in the starting point, which is in an abyss of water called Nun. The Nun stretched in all directions to form a kind of mini-Universe or proto-Universe from which the created Universe would emerge. The exact significance of this primeval ocean remains a mystery to Egyptologists, who cannot understand how, on the one hand, it could be attached physically to the earth (it was the source of the Nile). On the other hand, it formed the celestial ocean of the sky. In any event, all sources agree that the Nun had given birth to all things – the earth, the sky, the stars, the Sun, and the Moon.

The ancient Egyptians had many universal gods namely:

Ra – the sun god

Anubis as a jackal – the funerary god

Horus – the royal god (patron)

Maat – God of truth, justice and order

Shu – air god

Nut – sky goddess

Geb – god of earth

Osiris – god of earth and wind

Aten – the disc of the sun (god)

Amun – the supreme force of the cosmos

Ptah – intellectual god

Isis – goddess of protection, magic and personal salvation

The pharaoh Khenaten appointed Aten instead of the traditional pantheon, and called him as the creator and giver of life. The combination of Amun and Ra became one God (amun-Ra) who was the greatest visible force in nature.

The complexity refers to the fact that Egyptian religion never really was "a religion", but rather a universe of religions that often interacted, inspired each other, copied each other and often allowed one cult to dominate so that smaller cults disappeared or changed. Never was a unified theology defined and imposed on the many cult centres. The closest we get is the "monotheism" of Akhenaten in the 14th century BCE, but this orientation proved to be short lived.

In their myths, the air god Shu, assisted by other gods, holds up Nut, the sky, as Geb, the earth, lies beneath as seen in their archeology, Figure (63).

Figure (63): Representation of the universe by the ancient Egyptians

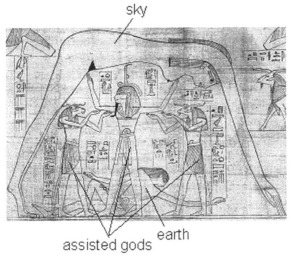

sky

assisted gods   earth

http://en.wikipedia.org/wiki/Ancient_Egyptian_religion

30.8 Hinduism

According to Western scholars, the religious tradition that we know as Hinduism is the product of at least 5,000 years of development, with roots stretching back to the Indus Valley civilization, which prospered some 4 - 5,000 years ago. However, the origins of this religion are shrouded in mystery and according to Hindu scriptures may be millions of years old. Hinduism does not have a historical founder, nor does it have a central authority for defining or imposing its beliefs and practices. Hinduism is not just a single religion, but a "mosaic of religion". Within it we can find most elementary superstitions and mythologies, from the cult of inanimate objects, like stones, rivers, planets to animate objects, like trees, animals, heroes, dead ancestors and spirits

With its cyclical notion of time, the Hindu tradition perceives that the material world is created not once but repeatedly, time and time again. The cosmos follows one cycle within a framework of cycles. It may have been created and may reach an end, but it represents only one turn in the perpetual "wheel of time", which revolves infinitely through successive cycles of creation and destruction. Additionally, this universe is considered to be one of many, all enclosed "like innumerable bubbles floating in space". Within this universe, there are three main regions: the heavenly planets, the earthly realm and the lower worlds. Within this cycle of creation and destruction of the universe, the soul (atman) also undergoes its own version of a cycle called samsara. It is the cycle of rebirth in which individual souls are repeatedly reincarnated.

Hinduism believes that this is not the first world, nor is it the first universe. There have been and will be many more worlds and universes than there are drops of water in the holy river Ganges. The universes are made by Lord Brahma the Creator, maintained by Lord Vishnu the Preserver and destroyed by Lord Shiva. Since the universes must be destroyed before they can be recreated, Lord Shiva is called the Destroyer and Re-creator. These three gods are all forms of the Supreme One and part of the Supreme One. The Supreme One is behind and beyond all.

After each old universe is destroyed nothing is left but a vast ocean. Floating on this ocean, resting on the great snake Ananta, is Lord Vishnu. Some say that a lotus flower springs from his navel and from this comes Lord Brahma. And it is from Lord Brahma that all creation comes.

Everything disappears into the Supreme One. For an unimaginable period of time chaos and water exist alone. Then once again Lord Vishnu appears, floating on the vast ocean. From Lord Vishnu comes forth Lord Brahma of the new universe and the cycle continues forever.

Hinduism believes in incarnation (the doctrine of reincarnation), known also with other terms like, rebirth, transmigration of the soul, *metempsychosis* (or more accurately, *metensomatosis,* "passage from one body to another"), *palingenesis* (Gr., lit., "to begin again"). It also concerns the rebirth of the soul or self in a series of physical or preternatural embodiments, which are customarily human or animal in nature but are in some instances divine, angelic, demonic, vegetative, or astrological.

30.9 Sikhism

Sikhism is a progressive religion that was well ahead of its time when it was founded over 500 years ago. The Sikh religion today has a following of over 20 million people worldwide and is ranked as the worlds 5th largest religion.

Sikhs believe that, for endless ages, there was only utter darkness (nothingness). There was no earth or sky, there was no day or night, no moon or sun; there was only the Lord (Akaal) Command. Only Akaal stayed in solitary meditation.

The existence of the universe and the design or pattern behind it makes people feel that it could not "just have happened", that there is a Great Designer. Just as a big mansion cannot be built without a master-builder or architect, the universe must have been created by a Master-Designer who we designate as God. For Sikhism, God is both in and above the universe. God is the Whole and the world a part of that Whole.

A complete knowledge of God is impossible. The Guru Nanak says, "Only one who is as great as He, can know Him fully." We can only have some glimpses of Him from His works. The universe is His sport in which He takes delight. The world is a play of the Infinite in the field of the finite. He has created an infinite number of worlds and constellations. The world in which we live is a small atom as compared to other worlds.

They believe that guru jee (the main Lord) says "keetaa pasaao eko kavao". With his one word, the universe was created. Then what was the process? On panna 1037-38 Satguru describes that the elements of air and water were evolved along with everything else in the universe. On panna 19, Satguru says "sache te pavanaa bhaiyaa pavne te jal hoi. jal tay tribhavan saajiyaa, ghat ghat jot samoi" from the true one, air (gases) was created and from them was created water. From water arose the three worlds (metaphor or common term for the universe and all within) with his divine light within all bodies. This is how the universe and all life were created.

30.10 Sumerian Creation Myth

Sumerian civilization (3500-1750 B.C.) originated in what is now southern Iraq, just upriver from the mouths of the Tigris and Euphrates rivers.

In Sumerian Mythology there was a pantheon of good and evil gods and goddesses who came to Earth to create the human race. According to some resources, these gods came from Nibru - 'Planet of the Crossing.' The Assyrians and Babylonians called it 'Marduk', after their chief god. Sumerians said one year on planet Nibiru, a sar, was equivalent in time to 3,600 Earth years. Anunnaki lifespans were 120 sars which is 120 x 3,600 or 432,000 years. According to the King List - 120 sars had passed from the time the Anunnaki arrived on Earth to the time of the Flood.

Religion was largely centered on several myths and mysteries. The principle myths were:

The Creation of the World

The Apocalypse (the Flood)

The Descent of Inanna

The Myth of the Slain King

The Wedding of Inanna and Dumuzi (the Sacred Marriage rite)

Sumerian astronomy was primitive compared to later Babylonian standards. They recognized and cataloged the brightest stars, outlined a rudimentary set of Zodiacal constellations, and noted the movements of the five visible planets (Mercury, Venus, Mars, Jupiter, and Saturn), as well as the Sun and Moon amongst the stars of the Zodiac. They also developed a rudimentary system of astrological divination for use in foreseeing the future of city-states and battles, but not for predicting personal futures. Their calendar was lunar, consisting of 12 lunar months or a 354 day lunar year. Each month began on the New Moon. Actually, the month began at sunset, with the first visible (thinnest) crescent of the New Moon.

Their myths are similar to the Babylonians in that Heaven and Earth were once a mountain that rose out of the primeval Sea. The mountain's peak reached into Heaven and its base was the Earth. An was heaven, and Ki was Earth. Nammu is the Sea goddess that surrounded the Earth. She was also the original dark chaos out of which everything formed. The mountain rose up out of the blackness of the deep sea. Enlil, the Air god, seperated Heaven and Earth and gave birth to the dawn. Enlil raped Ninlil the Air Goddess, and she gave birth to the Moon god, Nanna. Nanna and Ningal, his consort, gave birth to Utu, the Sun. Thus the Moon was born out of the darkness, before the Sun. This may be an indicator of the earlier matriarchal religion. Nanna and Ningal also gave birth to Inanna, the Evening Star.

Another myth according to "Gilgamesh, Enkidu, and the Netherworld", is that in the first days all needed things were created. Heaven and earth were separated. An took Heaven, Enlil took the earth, Ereshkigal was carried off to the netherworld as a prize, and Enki sailed off after her.

30.11 Yazidism

The Yazidis are members of both Kurdish and Islamic Sufi religions. Their roots descend form Indo-Iranian backgrounds. They are primarily a Kurdish-speaking people living in the Mosul region of northern Iraq, with additional communities in Transcaucasia, Turkey, Syria, and Armenia. The Yazidis believe in God as creator of the universe, which takes care of seven holy beings or angels, the most influential is angel Melek Tauoos, the Peacock Angel.

Their whole origins story makes Melek Tauoos, the archangel they worship to be a good version of the devil. They praise him for not bowing to Adam. Then God gave life to Adam from his own breath and instructed all archangels to bow to Adam. All the archangels obeyed, except for Tawûsê Melek. In answer to God, Tawûsê Melek replied, "How can I submit to another being! I am from your illumination while Adam is made of dust." Then God praised him and made him the leader of all angels and his deputy on the Earth.

The tale of the Yazidis' origin found in the Black Book gives them a distinctive ancestry and expresses their feeling of difference from other races. Before the roles of the sexes were determined, Adam and Eve quarreled about which of them provided the creative element in the begetting of children. Each stored their seed in a jar which was then sealed. When Eve's was opened it was full of insects and other unpleasant creatures, but inside Adam's jar was a beautiful boychild. This lovely child, known as *son of Jar* grew up to marry an *houri* and became the ancestor of the Yazidis. Therefore, the Yazidis are regarded as descending from Adam alone, while other humans are descendants of Adam and Eve, [Allison, Christine (2001). The Yazidi Oral Tradition in Iraqi Kurdistan, Psychology Press. p. 40, ISBN 0700713972].

Yazidis believe that in Northern Iraq there is a place called Lalish where the universe was born. A small conical monument sits in a courtyard in the center of Lalish. It represents heaven and earth. The round knob at the top is the sun.

Inside the cone are seven layers. Supposedly there are seven layers in the earth. A candle representing the life force of the universe burns inside. Candles are placed in wind-protected altars all around Lalish. The Yazidis keep the flames burning forever. Without fire, they say, all life would be extinguished.

31. The Actual Creation of the Universe Was a Miracle Not Explained by Natural Phenomenon.

Is there an intelligent creative power (supernatural) behind the existence of the "Laws of Nature"? These questions are beyond the scope of science and can only be discussed in the realm of philosophy and metaphysics (human imagination). Scientists can only; discover, examine and hypothesize on the physical laws of nature.

31.1 Quotations

1- It is often said that science must avoid any conclusions which beat the supernatural. This seems to me to be both bad logic and bad science. Science is not a game in which arbitrary rules are used to decide what explanations are to be permitted. Rather, it is an effort to make true statements about physical reality. It was only about sixty years ago that the expansion of the universe was first observed. This fact immediately suggested a singular event--that at some time in the distant past the universe began expanding from an extremely small size. Too many people only this inference was loaded with overtones of a supernatural event--the creation, the beginning of the universe. The prominent physicist A.S. Eddington probably spoke for many physicists when voicing his disgust with such a notion, as per Michael Behe, Professor of Biochemistry at Lehigh University. He continued to say:

"Philosophically, the notion of an abrupt beginning to the present order of Nature is repugnant to me, as I think it must be to most; and even those who would welcome a proof of the intervention of a Creator will probably consider that a single winding up at some remote epoch is not really the kind of relation between God and his world that brings satisfaction to the mind".

Nonetheless, the Big Bang hypothesis was embraced by physics and over the years has proven to be a very fruitful model. The point here is that physics followed the data where it seemed to lead, even though some thought the model gave aid and comfort to religion

2- We believe that the "bara/asah" of Genesis 1 implies God working through miracle and processes to effect creation. We believe that the "Yom" of Genesis I may be interpreted as either "day" or "epoch." In either case Genesis may still be interpreted to allow for the large total time of the creation of the earth and the planets indicated by geology and astronomy. This model, usually called progressive creationism, suggests that God created the major types of plant and animal life at various times in geological history in a miraculous way and then He worked through a process (God acting in His customary way) to develop the tremendous variety of plant and animal life we see today. To accept the compelling evidence for the geological age, it should not be equated with accepting the general theory of evolution (macroevolution).

Source: Article – The trustwortness od Scripture in Areas Relating to Natural Science. [A reprint of Chapter 5 (pp. 283-348) from Hermeneutics, Inerrancy, and the Bible, Radmacher and Preus, eds. (Zondervan, 1984)]

While these various nonradiometric methods of dating may be inaccurate for giving absolute ages, they occur at rates that give incontrovertible evidence that the earth is much older than ten thousand years. Furthermore, one cannot postulate here an uncertainty in assumptions as is done with radiometric dating, since no assumptions are involved. Unless God chose to create the universe with this clear impression of great antiquity, the earth must actually be quite old, (said by Walter Bradley, currently working with Baylor University's engineering department and is a fellow of the International Society for Complexity Information and Design). Walter Bradley has also performed seminal research in the origin of life.

3- The Big Bang and Hoyle's Steady State were mere abstractions, unable to be tested. Then, in 1964, Dr. Arno Penzias and Robert Wilson of Bell Labs encountered continuous static on certain microwave frequencies. Rotating their antenna in a vain attempt to remove the noise, they realized it was coming from all directions, permeating the universe. Physicists hailed this as the first observational evidence of the Big Bang known as "cosmic background radiation" or "the radio echo of creation."

Today, advocates of the Big Bang think that their theory is a substitute for God. However, it's just the opposite. Hoyle rejected the Big Bang in spite of the evidence because he knew that the Big Bang pointed irresistibly to the existence of God.

4- Moreover, the theist can muster credible reasons for belief in God. For example, one can argue that the contingency of the universe — in light of Big Bang cosmology, the expanding universe, and the second law of thermodynamics (which implies that the universe has been "wound up" and will eventually die a heat death) — demonstrate that the cosmos has not always been here. It could not have popped into existence uncaused, out of absolutely nothing, because we know that whatever begins to exist has a cause. A powerful first cause, like the God of theism, plausibly answers the question of the universe's origin. Also, the fine-tunedness of the universe — with complexly balanced conditions that seem tailored for life — points to the existence of an intelligent designer, (said by Paul Copan, the Pledger Family Chair of Philosophy and Ethics at Palm Beach Atlantic University, West Palm Beach, FL).

5- The history of the Big Bang model for well over three-quarters of a century has been one of radical predictions repeatedly, confirmed by the failure of every attempt. Some of them were extremely speculative, to avoid the absolute origin of the universe posited in the standard model. With each failure, the theory is corroborated anew. The defender of the Kalam cosmological argument seems to be on secure ground in appropriating the Big Bang theory as empirical confirmation of the beginning of the universe (said byWilliam Lane Craig, president of the Evangelical Philosophical Society and the Philosophy of Time Society).

6- Of course, there are many Creationists who argue for an old earth. Biblically, this position that the word for day is used for more than twenty-four hours even in Genesis 2:4, shows that the events of the sixth day surely took more than twenty-four hours, and Hebrews 4:4.5 implies that God is still in His seventh-day rest. If the seventh day can be long, then the others could too. Scientifically, this view does not require any novel theories to explain the evidence. One of the biggest problems for the young earth view is in astronomy. We can see light from stars that took 15 billion years to get here. To say that God created them with the appearance of age does not satisfy the question of how their light reached us. We have watched star explosions that happened billions of years ago, but if the universe is not billions of years old, then we are seeing light from stars that never existed because they would have died before the creation. Why would God deceive us with the evidence? The old earth view seems to fit the evidence better and causes no problem with the bible (said by Norman Geisler, President of Southern Evangelical Seminary, in Charlotte, North Carolina).

7- For centuries, people searched for an answer to the question of "how the universe came into being". Thousands of models of the universe have been put forward and thousands of theories have been produced throughout history. However, a review of these theories reveals that they all have at their core one of two different models. The first is the concept of an infinite universe without beginning, which no longer has any scientific basis. The second is that the universe was created from nothing, which is currently recognized by the scientific community as "the standard model", The first model, which has proven not to be viable, defended the proposition that the universe has existed for an infinite amount of time and will exist endlessly in its current state. This idea of an infinite universe was developed in ancient Greece, and made its way to the western world as a product of the materialistic philosophy that was revived with Renaissance. At the core of the Renaissance is a re-examination of the works of ancient Greek thinkers. Thus, materialist philosophy and the concept of an infinite universe defended by this philosophy were taken off the dusty shelves of history because of philosophical and ideological concerns and presented to people as if they were scientific facts (from the work of Harun Yahya, Zakir Naik, and Caner Taslaman).

This is one of the powerful secrets of Sabbath. When the Holy One originally created the world, He only endowed creation with sufficient power to last for six days, for reasons known only to Him (but also somewhat revealed to those who have merited to study these mysteries). Then He created Shabbat, and on this day G-d restores and revives the world's soul, enabling it to carry on with the burden of existence for another six days. Thus, the process continues throughout the ages, and through Shabbat, the world is constantly renewed, and given a new lease on life.

32. Belief That Only Science Can Deliver Supreme Knowledge on the Universe Is Doubtful at Best

32.1 Our Planets Do Not Depend on the Prior Creation of Our Sun

32.1.1 Euler Method

There are many methods to solve rotation curves using different approximation methods of first and second order differential equations. The methods are: Euler's Method, Modified Euler's Method, Heun's Method, Taylor's Method, Runge-Kutta Method, Adams-Bashforth Moulton Method, and Milne-Simpson Method. The simplest method is the modified Euler Method, where as Runge-Kutta is the most accurate one. Therefore the Euler method is used for this analysis.

Why do we use Euler method in this calculation? Let's take the rotation of the nearest satellite to the earth which is the moon. The orbit of the moon is elliptical with an eccentricity of about 0.0549. The non-circular form of the lunar orbit makes variations in the moon's angular speed and its apparent dimension as it moves towards and away from an observer on earth. The mean angular daily movement, relative to an imaginary observer at the barycenter, is 13.176357° to the east. The direction of the orbit is not permanent in space, but precesses over time. One motion is the precession of the line of apsides. The ellipse of the lunar orbit slowly rotates counterclockwise, and completes a full revolution in about 8.850 years. The other movement is clockwise, where, the precession of the orbital plane itself is about an axis perpendicular to the ecliptic. The points where the lunar orbit intersects the ecliptic (the nods) presses with time and speed, completing one revolution in about 18.6 years. When the moon is at its perigee (the closest point to the earth) its rotation is slower than its orbital motion at any other point and it reaches it maximum speed when it is outermost from the earth (this is called apogee).

We shall use the Euler Number e of the value 2.718 (approximately), as e gives the maximum and accurate curvature of a rotation of a planet, where dy/dt at t(0) = 1. At this point the tangent of the curve = x/y =1, and when x =1, y will equal 2 for n = ∞ only for the tangent of the e curve. But for ∞ the curve will reach 2.718, i.e.; when $(1+1/n)^n = yn = \infty$.

The more the number of intervals starting from point y(t),when t = 0, and e =1, therefore,the curve will take the shape of this formula:

$$z = (x^2 + y^2)^{1/2} \exp (j\tan^{-1} (y / x)), \text{ or}$$

$$\ln(z) = \ln((x^2+y^2)^{1/2} \cdot e^{j\tan-1y/x})$$

$$= \ln(x^2+y^2)^{1/2} + \ln (e^{j\tan-1y/x})$$

$$= \tfrac{1}{2}(\ln{(x^2+y^2)}) + j\tan^{-1}(x/y).$$

Considering $x = 3$, and $y = 4$, the length of the curve tangent will be 5, where as the length of the curve would be 5.6 due to e.

If $\tan^{-1}x/y$ denoted by θ, then the last equation can be written as:

$C \cdot e^{j(\omega t + \theta)}$, where $\omega = 2\pi f$, and f is the frequency of rotation, $\pi = 3.142857$. C is a constant.

Now we will assume the following movements:
- Spinning of earth around itself,
- Rotation of earth around the sun,
- Rotation of the sun within the galaxy Milky Way,
- Rotation of the Milky Way with respect to the universe.

And let's assume:
Mass of the Earth   Me
Mass of Sun   Ms
Mass of Milky Way   Mm
We shall consider the earth spinning takes the formula $\tilde{M}es = Me \cdot e^{j(\omega_e t + \theta_e)}$, where t is the position of the earth spinning after a start (hypothetical), and θe is not 23.5°, but it is the angle of a certain point on earth with respect to global equator. The rotation of the earth around the sun would be $\tilde{M}es = Me \cdot e^{j(\omega_e t + \theta_{es})}$ where θes is the angle at which the earth rotation around the sun is displaced from the sun orbit. Similarly, the rotation of the sun with respect to its galaxy (Milky Way) would be $\tilde{M}s = Ms \cdot e^{j(\omega_s t + \theta_{sm})}$, and the rotation of the milky way with respect to the universe would be $\tilde{M}m = Mm \cdot e^{j(\omega_m t + \theta_{mu})}$.

Now the earth position to the universe can be represented by:

$Mp\, \theta e \propto Me \cdot e^{j(\omega_e t + \theta_e)} \times Me \cdot e^{j(\omega_e t + \theta_{es})} \times Ms \cdot e^{j(\omega_s t + \theta_{sm})} \times Mm \cdot e^{j(\omega_m t + \theta_{mu})}$, where Mp is the position of the earth at time t. Then when constants equal constants and variables equals variables, one can get:

Mp = C1 x Me x Ms x Mm, and   (1)
θe = C2 x θe x θes x θsm x θmu (2)

The inclination (tilting) of the sun orbit in the Orion Arm does not change the above formula (Equating 2 above), where:

$e^{j\theta_{sm}} = \lim_{n=\infty} \cdot (1 + e^{j\theta_{sm}}/n)^n$. When $n = \infty$, then $e^{j\theta_{sm}}$ = constant.

in other words,

$e^{j\Theta_{sm}} = \cos\Theta_{sm} + j\sin\Theta_{sm}$ and since $e^{j\Theta_{sm}}$ is constant, then $j\sin\Theta_{sm}$ is constant, when $\cos\Theta_{sm}$ is fixed, which is the case.

Other planets will have similar formulas.
This would conclude that if the sun died out after five billion years as estimated by scientists, then it would be converted to another planet, terrestrial satellite or a black hole, but with a certain mass. Whatever the size of the dead sun is, it would have a mass. Accordingly, Mp will never ever be zero. That means that if the sun died, the earth and the planets would still be there in their places or they could be converted to another type of planet and would be associated with another star with a different displacement and speed. This concludes the idea that the earth would be created without the sun. Similarly, other planets associated with the sun do not depend on the prior creation of the sun; they might be created before the creation of the sun. If scientists do not know the future of our planets, they also do not know the birth and the beginning of the universe. Therefore, the theory of Big Bang and other hypotheses are uncertain.

32.1.2 Angular Momentum

Newton demonstrated that the position and the momentum of an object such as the moon at any given time determine its position and momentum at any subsequent time, as long as it travels freely. The position and momentum of the moon at a given time - its "initial state" - determines the position and momentum of the moon at every subsequent time, whether or not we know this initial state. Also, if we know its initial state, then using Newton's laws of motion we can predict the moon's future states. Knowing the position and momentum of the moon along with knowing the position and momentum of the earth as it revolves around the sun, is what makes it possible to form tide tables for years, decades, and even centuries in the future. The same principle can be used to correlate the position and momentum of the sun with the position and momentum of the planets of the sun. This means that a variation in the position and momentum of the Sun will affect the position of its planets, and this is a natural a linear variation between the sun and its planets. Mathematically,

Position of the Sun = Position of the planets
Momentum of the Sun = Momentum of the planets

Since all planets and the sun rotate in basic orbits, the momentum in the previous formula is replaced by the angular momentum

Angular momentum of the Sun = Angular Momentum of the planets

Since the position is controlled by mass and speed, and the angular momentum also depends on mass and speed, we shall consider the angular momentum in our calculation.

To calculate the angular momentum we need to know the mass, velocity, and radius of the sun and each planet as shown in the following table:

	Mass	Radius	Velocity
Mercury	3.28E+23	6E+07	47.89
Venus	5.07E+24	1.05E+08	35.03
Earth	5.97E+24	1.5E+08	29.78
Mars	6.39E+23	2.25E+08	24.13
Jupiter	1.90E+27	7.8E+08	13.06
Saturn	5.67E+26	1.38E+09	9.64
Uranus	8.36E+25	2.94E+09	6.81
Neptune	1.01E+26	4.5E+09	5.43
Pluto	1.25E+22	5.7E+09	4.74
Sun	1.99E+30	2.4598E+17	22000

Where mass is in kilograms, radius is (between the planets and the sun, as well as is the distance from the Sun to the centre of the Milky Way Galaxy) in kilometers, and velocity is in kilometers per second.
The angular momentum is equal to:

L (Angular Momentum) = M (Mass) . R (Radius) . V(Velocity)

L (for all planets) = $3.109E+37 \ kgkm^2/s$
L (for the Sun)   = $1.0769E+52 \ kgkm^2/s$

From the above results, one can see that the sun can drive more planets around its orbit.
In other words, the planets are orbiting the sun, but not under the influence of the sun, since L sun > L planets. Our sun influences other planets orbiting another star, or our planets are influenced, in addition to our sun, by another star. The conclusion is that our planets are not restricted to the sole authority of our sun. It also could mean that our planets were not necessarily born as a result of the explosion of the sun, or created simultaneously with the sun.

32.1.3 Gravitational Attraction

Now we will evaluate the gravitational attraction between the Sun and the Galaxy (Milky Way), and the gravitational attraction between the sun and all its planets. Scientifically, they should be equal. If not, then there is no equilibrium between the attraction between the sun and the planets.

Using Newton's Theory of Universal Gravitation which states that two objects will attract each other with a force proportional to their masses and inversely proportional to the square of distance between them. The Universal Gravity Equation is:

$F = GMm/R^2$

G as a constant equals 6.67 x 10 $^{-11}$. We will consider the Mass of the Milky Way(M) as 600 billion solar mass (helium gas mass). We don't consider the mass of the Milky Way within the halo as it is not as effective as the Hi gas. The sun mass(m) is equal to 1.99E+30 kg, and the distance between the sun and the Milky Way is
2.45981E+17 km. The calculations show that the gravitational attraction between the sun and the Milky Way is 6.44291E+40, whereas the gravitational attraction between the sun and all its orbiting planets is 5.66009E+28 Newtons. So the question is where is such a huge difference of force implemented? Do you know or God does know?

To conclude, there is imbalance in angular momentum, in attraction force and between the sun and its solar planets. The analysis also demonstrates that the earth and the solar planets are not conjoined to the sun in their spinning. Therefore, the analysis in this book reinforces theology over science.

32.2 The Cosmic Background Radiation (CBR) Is Misleading

Science suggests that there is a very low energy and very uniform radiation that we see filling the Universe. This is called the 3 Degree Kelvin Background Radiation, or the Microwave Background. This means that the universe is almost completely uniform because of the highly isotropic nature of the cosmic background radiation. However, it was indicated the universe if not uniform for two scientific reasons:

When we look at the microwave background coming from widely separated parts of the sky, it can be shown that these regions are too separated (due to the red shift and blue shift) to have been able to communicate with each other even with signals traveling at light velocity. Thus, how did they know to have a uniformed universe where the temperature is not the same? This general problem is called the horizon problem.

If the science proves that the present universe (on a very large scale) is homogenous and isotropic, therefore it is a uniform, small scale universe like superclusters which are not uniform because a quite lumpy CBR is shown in many regions of this small universe. This contradicts the uniformity of the universe and contradicts the Big Bang Theory.

32.3 Non-relativistic Matter Is Doubtful

The early universe was dominated by radiation, and after the Big Bang, the radiation converted to non-relativistic matter, i.e., the universe is primarily contained in massive matter of an average velocity much less than the speed of light. The early universe was radiation dominated, but the present universe is matter dominated. However, the matter created by and during the Big Bang is not in the form we see today. The matter in the universe that we see now is in the form of unseen or dark matter (cannot be seen by even the most sophisticated astronomical devices). Does the dark matter, which makes up 25% of the universe, have gravity and density different than the matter we know? Is the gold and silver on earth the same in the universe? The dark matter is one of the most important unsolved problems in science.

32.4 Relativistic Matter Is Also Doubtful

If the total energy produced by the three neutrinos (electron neutrinos, muon neutinos and tau neutrinos) exceeded an average of 50 electronvolts per neutrino, the whole universe would be made of mass without energy. This would result in the collapse of the universe. On the other hand, if the energy produced by the neutrinos is very small as it was proven (the energy produced from the cosmic background radiation like a galaxy survey, the Lyman-alpha forest and other infrared cosmic radiation) to be equal to less than 0.3 electronvolts [A. Goobar, S. Hannestad, E. Mörtsell, H. Tu (2006). "The neutrino mass bound from WMAP 3 year data, the baryon acoustic peak, the SNLS supernovae and the Lyman-α forest"], the universe would then be made only from energy. If this were true then no life and no planets would exist.

32.5 Where and When Did the Planck Era Happen?

The advocates of the Big Bang Theory suggested that at 1/100 seconds after the occurrence of the Big Bang, neutrinos were combining with neutrons to form electrons and protons. This means that atoms and matter were formed at that instant. The atom diameter is about 10^{-8} cm and the Planck length is 1.6 x 10^{-33} cm. If we look to the chronological order of the stages of the Big Bang, we conclude the following:

If the universe was flat, which it was during the first second after the Big Bang, the quantum mechanics would be used according to the Planck scale, and therefore there would be no atoms or matters. So, how the universe was expanding during the first second without matter!

Let's assume there was no matter during the Planck Era, and assume only neutrons were there. The neutrons beta decay could not be converted to protons. This is because it is the era of very high temperatures (1.4 x 10^{32} K). This could be true due to the decay of energy to neutrons, positrons (e^+) and electron neutrinos as shown below:

Energy -> n +e^+ + ve

Positrons produce electrons if they release or combine with photons. Therefore, a cycle of production of both electrons and positrons that might annihilate each other will happen. The product of this is energy, which is added to the original energy. The product would be an exponential increase in the energy to the first instant of the Big Bang. If this is true, we are still living in a bigger Big Bang that could destroy even the present universe.

32.6 The Dark Matter Concept That Causes Repulsion. Acceleration of the Expansion of the Universe Is Uncertain

Theorists have conceived that dark matter and dark energy cause the acceleration of the expansion of the universe. Acceleration can not be accomplished unless there is a repulsion force. Dark matter is fundamental particles that consist of electrons and positrons, (these two always in pair and attracts each other). The percentage of dark matter of the universe is 25%, which is considered a large number to attract, align, and bind one another. Also, dark matter is matter that does not interact electromagnetically but still reacts gravitationally. Because it does not interact with electromagnetic radiation (light. radio, infrared, etc), we can not detect it by these means; it is invisible.

But, based on transparent imaging of the universe, the gap between dark matters is unbelievably wide, like a person shouting to another person 1,000 miles away. How can there be binding or repulsion to cause the acceleration of the expansion of the universe. Thus, the dark matter concept that causes repulsion, proves that the acceleration of the expansion of the universe is doubtful. Dark matter would explain why galaxies hold together even though they spin too fast, but not accelerate the expansion of the universe.

32.7 The Inflation Theory Is a Joke

When theorists suggested that the Big Bang theory maintains that the universe was born about 15 billion years ago from a cosmological singularity (nothingness), they assumed that the start of the universe was in an infinite density and temperature. Opponents of the Big Bang theory dismissed the infinity of density and temperature as this could not be spoken in physical and thermodynamical terms. Instead, theorists invented the inflation theory, in which the cosmos became exponentially large within an infinitesimal fraction of a second. A group of theorists asserted that the universe started with one firing ball which became a huge, growing unshaped structure. Another group suggested that the universe started with many inflated firing balls that produced new balls, which in turn produce more balls, infinitely. If the latter inflation theory is correct, then the shape of the universe would be humped rather than opened or closed as previously thought. The humped universe was behind the new theory that the universe is in continuous oscillation. Some theorists called it "an oscillatory universe".

32.8 Do the Gravity and the Vacuum Energy Cause the Universe to Go Back to Its Singularity state?

The effects of vacuum energy can be observed in various phenomena such as spontaneous emission, the Casmir effect, the van der Waals bonds and the Lamb shift. It is thought that the vacuum energy could have influence on the sape of the universe and its expansion.

Quantum physics points out that vacuum energy has subatomic particles that are constantly being created and destroyed, but the resultant energy is not zero.

The observed accelerated expansion of the universe indicates the presence of vacuum energy corresponding to energy of about 104eV per centimeter cubed [A. Riess et al., Astrophys. J. 607, 665 (2004)]. The vacuum energy is accompanied by substantial negative pressure.

The gravitational field, which defines the metric and curvature of spacetime, is determined by the sum of all forms of energy and momentum. It was found that the gravity is not just the mass-energy density but actually the energy density plus three times the pressure as per the following formula:

$$G = Ve + 3Vp$$

Where G is the gravity, Ve is the vacuum energy and Vp is the vacuum pressure.

It is the Ve or the Vp that determines whether the gravity is attractive or repulsive. In the Friedmann-Lemaitre-Robertson-Walker metric, it can be shown that a strong constant negative pressure in all the universe causes an acceleration in universe expansion if the universe is already expanding, or a deceleration in universe contraction if the universe is already contracting. In fact, a negative pressure does not influence the gravitational interaction between masses — which remains attractive. If the vacuum energy has a negative pressure that does not influence the gravity, it means that G is influenced only by Ve and G becomes attractive. Therefore, the universe is contracting.

32.9 Are Black Holes Decay and Gravity Responsible for the Expansion?

In modern cosmology, it is conjectured that that there are always light "elementary" electric and magnetic objects with a mass/charge ratio smaller than the corresponding ratio for macroscopic extremal black holes, allowing extremal black holes to decay [Nima Arkani-hamed and others]. If this is true, then there is no need for 'mysterious dark matter' or Einstein's cosmological constant, which is a repulsive force explaining the expansion of the universe. In that case, the gravity is the only repulsive force (the resultant of the forces exerted by all the material objects in the universe seeking to occupy as large a space as possible) responsible for the expansion. The gravity force will then stabilize and compromise quantum mechanics and general relativity (even beyond the Planck scale) and render the string theory (or its modernized form M-theory) no longer valid. This will also emphasize that no one really knows what the background energy or even the bulk of the matter (created from energy) in the universe could possibly be.

32.10 Does Dark Matter Really Come from Neutrinos?

Some astronomers believe that dark matter comes from the mass of neutrinos. They derive weakly interacting massive particles or WIMPs, with which hypothetical particles are serving as one possible solution to the dark matter problem. These particles interact through the weak nuclear force and gravity. The weak force produces electrons and neutrinos when neutrons decay to protons.

The Sudbury Neutrino Observatory in Canada demonstrated that neutrinos are capable of oscillating between Lepton flavours (electron, tau and muon). This can only happen if one or more of the neutrino flavours does have mass. This contradicts the standard model of particle physics where flavours of electrons, taus and muons are much heavier than corresponding neutrinos, see table (5).

Table (5): Mass of leptons flavour

Leptons flavor	Mass (GeV)
Electron (e-)	5.11×10^{-4}
Electron neutrino	$< 10^{-8}$
Muon (μ-)	0.106
Muon neutrino	$< 3 \times 10^{-4}$
Tau (τ-)	1.78
Tau neutrino	$< 3.3 \times 10^{-2}$

Neutrinos are weakly interacting particles that were almost created in great abundance during the Big Bang. These neutrinos fill the universe including the earth, and yet are almost impossible to detect. Because neutrinos, which are discovered in particle accelerators and nuclear reactors, have negligible mass (The weight ratio of a neutrino to a 1kg bag of sugar is the same as the ratio of a grain of sand to the weight of the earth!), it is unlikely they make up much of the dark matter. The experiments of earlier twentieth-century scientists repeatedly indicated that neutrinos did not have mass (the speed of neutrinos could not be distinguished from that of light. According to relativity, particles such as photons that travel at the speed of light have zero masses. This reinforced the idea that neutrinos might have zero mass), although the Japanese-U.S. research team called the Super-Kamiokande Collaboration announced experiment results in 1998 that proved that neutrinos do indeed have mass.

Although inflation has many attractive features, it is not yet a proven theory because many of the details still do not work out right in realistic calculations without making assumptions that are poorly justified. Probably most cosmologists today believe inflation to be correct at least in its outlines, but further investigation will be required to establish whether this is indeed so. Conclusion

Looking at evidence, explanations, rationalizations, and arguments for naturalistic origins of the universe leads to a simple conclusion. Once all of the cards are on the table, recent discoveries have given life to interpretations that are long on theory and short on proof. To put it another way, all scientists have really proven about the origin of the universe is that they don't really know how it happened, and they may be looking at it the wrong way. Conclusion
http://www.allaboutcreation.org/steady-state-theory-faq.htm

33. Most Famous Scientists Believe in God

The Most Famous Scientists in Science and Technology (Not Scientists in Humanities) Believe in God. The Following Scientists and Dignitary People Are Just Few of Them.

1. Albert Einstein (German theoretical physicist, philosoper and author. He is known for his general relativity theory) said "My religion consists of a humble admiration of the illimitable superior spirit who reveals himself in the slight details we are able to perceive with our frail and feeble mind." He said "I do not believe in a personal God and I have never denied this but have expressed it clearly. If something is in me which can be called religious then it is the unbounded admiration for the structure of the world so far as our science can reveal it." "I, at any rate, am convinced that He does not throw dice." -- in a 1926 letter to Max Born. Einstein's famous epithet on the "uncertainty principle" was "God does not play dice" - and to him this was a real statement about a God in whom he believed. A famous saying of his was "Science without religion is lame, religion without science is blind."

2. Isaac Newton (English physicist, mathematician, astronomer, natural philosopher, alchemist, and theologian) was devoutly religious and saw numbers as involved in understanding God's plan for history from the Bible. He did considerable work on biblical numerology, and, though aspects of his beliefs were not orthodox, he thought theology was very important. In his system of physics, God is essential to the nature and absoluteness of space. In Principia he stated, "The most beautiful

system of the sun, planets, and comets, could only proceed from the counsel and dominion on an intelligent and powerful Being."

3. Richard Feynman (Noble Prize winner in quantum electrodynamics physics) – "Many scientists do believe in both science and God, the God of revelation, in a perfectly consistent way."

4. Max Planck (German physicist and founder of quantum theory) expressed in his 1937 lecture "Religion and Naturwissenschaft," his view that God is everywhere, and held that "the holiness of the unintelligible Godhead is conveyed by the holiness of symbols." Atheists, he thought, attach too much importance to what are merely symbols. Planck was a churchwarden from 1920 until his death, and believed in an almighty, all-knowing, beneficent God (though not necessarily a personal one). Both science and religion wage a "tireless battle against skepticism and dogmatism, against unbelief and superstition" with the goal "toward God!"

5. Johannes Kepler (German mathematician, astronomer and astrologer) was an extremely sincere and pious Lutheran, whose works on astronomy contain writings about how space and the heavenly bodies represent the Trinity. Kepler suffered no persecution for his open avowal of the sun-centered system, and, indeed, was allowed as a Protestant to stay in Catholic Graz as a Professor for five years when other Protestants had been expelled! Kipler said on God "I was merely thinking God's thoughts after him. Since we astronomers are priests of the highest God in regard to the book of nature "it benefits us to be thoughtful, not of the glory of our minds, but rather, above all else, of the glory of God."

6. Galileo Galilei (Italian physicist. mathematician, astronomer and philosopher) expressly said that the Bible cannot err, and saw his system (his controversial work on the solar system) as an alternate interpretation of the biblical texts.

7. Robert Boyle (Irish natural philosopher, chemist, physicist, and inventor) wrote in The Christian Virtuoso that the study of nature was a central religious duty. Boyle wrote against atheists in his day (the notion that atheism is a modern invention is a myth), and was clearly much more devoutly religious than the average in his era.

8. Michael Faraday (English chemist and physicist) was a devoutly Christian member of the Sandemanians, which significantly influenced him and strongly affected the way in which he approached and interpreted nature. Originating from Presbyterians, the Sandemanians rejected the idea of state churches, and tried to go back to a New Testament type of Christianity.

9. William Thomson Kelvin (British scientist) was a very committed Christian, who was certainly more religious than the average for his era in an era when many were nominal, apathetic, or anti-Christian.

10. Gregor Mendel (Austrain monk and scientists) was called the father of genetics. He began his research in 1856 (three years before Darwin published his Origin of Species) in the garden of the Monastery in which he was a monk. Mendel was elected Abbot of his Monastery in 1868.

11. Rene Descartes (French mathematician) had a deep religious faith as a Roman Catholic, which he retained to his dying day. God is central to his whole philosophy. What he really wanted to see was that his philosophy be adopted as standard Roman Catholic teaching. Rene Descartes and Francis Bacon are generally regarded as the key figures in the development of scientific methodology. Both had systems in which God was important, and both seem more devout than the average for their era.

12. Sir Francis Bacon (English philosopher, statesman, scientist, lawyer, jurist and author) established his goals as being the discovery of truth, service to his country, and service to the church. Although his work was based upon experimentation and reasoning, he rejected atheism as being the result of insufficient depth of philosophy, stating, "It is true, that a little philosophy inclineth man's mind to atheism, but depth in philosophy bringeth men's minds about to religion; for while the mind of man looketh upon second causes scattered, it may sometimes rest in them, and go no further; but when it beholdeth the chain of them confederate, and linked together, it must needs fly to Providence and Deity."

13. Nicholas Copernicus (Polish astronomer) attended various European universities, and became a Canon in the Catholic Church. He referred to God in many of his publications.

14. Mohammed Abdus Salam (a Pakistani theoretical physicist, astrophysicist and Noble laureate in physics) was a devout Muslim, who saw his religion as integral to his scientific work. He once wrote: "The Holy Quran enjoins us to reflect on the verities of Allah's created laws of nature; however, that our generation has been privileged to glimpse a part of His design is a bounty and a grace for which I render thanks with a humble heart".

15. Abdulla Badawi (Malaysian Prime Minister) was a well-respected religious leader and nationalist, and was one of the founding members of Hizbul Muslimin, later known as PAS. After independence, Syeikh Abdullah became the first mufti of Penang after Independence.

16. Ahmed Zewail (Egyptian-American scientist, and the winner of the 1999 Noble Prize in Chemistry for his work on femtochemistry) grew up in a very religious atmosphere defined in his early childhood. Sidi Ibrahim El-

Desouqi was of a paramount significance in Zewail's childhood. He used to go to the mosque a few meters from his house not only to pray, but also to study because the mosque is this spiritual place not just for prayer. In Dusuq the famous mosque of Sidi Ibrahim El-Desouqi was like a glue to keep everyone praying, working, and even living together in harmony.

17. Charles Darwin is an English naturalist who established that all species of life have descended over time from common ancestors, and proposed the scientific theory that this branching pattern of evolution resulted from a process that he called natural selection). Though he thought of religion as a tribal survival strategy, Darwin still believed that God was the ultimate lawgiver. The "Lady Hope Story", published in 1915, claimed that Darwin had reverted back to Christianity on his sickbed. The Lady Hope Story first appeared in an American Baptist newspaper the Watchman Examiner on 15 August 1915, preceded by a four-page report on a summer Bible conference held in Northfield, which year ran from 30 July to 15 August 1915. In the Lady Hope Story, it was stated that Darwin, before he died, waved his hand toward the window as he pointed out the scene beyond, while in the other hand he held an open Bible, which he was always studying. Then, placing his finger on certain passages, he commented on them.

I made some allusions to the strong opinions expressed by many persons on the history of the creation, its grandeur, and then their treatment of the earlier chapters of the Book of Genesis.

He seemed greatly distressed, his fingers twitched nervously, and a look of agony came over his face as he said: "I was a young man with unformed ideas. I threw out queries, suggestions, wondering all the time over everything, and to my astonishment, the ideas took like wildfire. People made a religion of them."

Then he paused, and after a few more sentences on "the holiness of God" and the "grandeur of this book," looking at the Bible which he was holding tenderly all the time, he suddenly said: "I have a summer house in the garden which holds about thirty people. It is over there," pointing through the open window. "I want you very much to speak there. I know you read the Bible in the villages. To-morrow afternoon I should like the servants on the place, some tenants and a few of the neighbours; to gather there. Will you speak to them?"

"What shall I speak about?" I asked.

"Christ Jesus!" he replied in a clear, emphatic voice, adding in a lower tone, "and his salvation. Is not that the best theme? And then I want you to sing some hymns with them. You lead on your small instrument, do you not?" The wonderful look of brightness and animation on his face as he said this I shall never forget, for he added: "If you take the meeting at three o'clock this window will be open, and you will know that I am joining in with the singing". See Collection: Avijit Roy, Published on Darwin Day (February 12, 2006).

18. Dr. Arthur H. Compton, Nobel Laureate (Physics) for his discovery of the Compton effect which provided the final confirmation of the validity of Planck's quantum hypothesis said,
"It is not difficult for me to have this faith, for it is incontrovertible that where there is a plan there is intelligence - an orderly, unfolding universe testifies to the truth of the most majestic statement ever uttered - 'In the beginning, God."

19. Charles Hard Townes, Nobel Prize winner in physics for fundamental work in the field of quantum electronics said,
"The question of science seems to be unanswered if we explore from science alone. Thus I believe there is a need for some metaphysical or religious explanation. I believe in the concept of God an in his existence." "To me, God is personal yet omnipresent - a great source of strength Who has made an enormous difference to me".

20. Arthur Leonard Schawlow, Nobel prize winner and professor from Stanford University for his contribution to the development of laser spectroscopy said,
"We are fortunate to have the Bible which tells us so much about God in widely accessible terms." When commenting about the universe and wonders of life he stated "The only possible answers are religious.....I find a need for God in the universe and in my life".

21. Alan Sandage, the world's greatest observational cosmologist from the Observatories of the Carnegie Institution, won a prize given by Swedish parliament equivalent to Nobel prize (there is no Nobel prize for cosmology) and became a Christian after being a scientist.
"The nature of God is not found in any part of science, for that we must turn to the scriptures." He also writes that the Big Bang can only be understood as "a miracle." In a lecture by Fritz Shafer from a website by Leadership University:
http://www.leaderu.com/realri9501/bingbang2.html

22. William Phillips, co-recipient of the 1997 Nobel Prize in Physics for development of methods to cool and trap atoms with laser light, Works for the US National Institute of Standards and Technology said,
"I said something like, 'There are many people I want to thank, and I'd also like to thank God for giving us such a wonderful and interesting universe to explore."

Some other spiritual & religious leaders include: Ayatollah Ruhollah Khomeini, Dalai Lama, Desmond Tutu, Martin Luther, Martin Luther King Jr., Mary Baker Eddy, Mother Teresa, Mary Baker Eddy, Harun Yahia, and others.

Atheist scholars contend that science continuously reveals religious beliefs to be "the hideous fantasies of a prior age" (as author Sam Harris put it).

However, science may actually be closer to suggesting just the opposite. Modern science suggests that extra dimensions of space and perhaps even whole parallel universes exist, that some things don't have physical form until you look at them, that a particle can be in two places at once because it bounces back and forth in space AND time, and that events on Earth can be influenced instantaneously by events deep in the cosmos. Even Max Planck, the Nobel Prize winning physicist who was the father of quantum physics, came to believe that all matter is an illusion. "Indeed, not only is science incapable of disproving God, it is increasingly revealing that our universe is so bizarre that refutation of the possibility of God has become the naïve perspective. Moreover, as I discuss in this book, it seems quite likely that God does intend for us to employ science in order to glean at least a glimpse of what lies beyond our immediate universe."

34. Comments by the Author

The universe is huge and its timeline is much, much longer than our galaxy (the Milky Way). Because of this, scientists and cosmologists can't understand with certainty how the universe began or how it will end. They can, however, collect evidence, make educated guesses and establish theories. They are currently engaged in a hot debate. The first group says the universe will go to the Big Crunch and return to its singularity point; the second group says the universe will expand forever and the third group says it will go into transition from the Big Bang to the Big Crunch and back to the Big Bang and the cycle will continue in a span of billions of years.

34.1 Temperatures of the Universe Expansion Appear to Be Inconsistent

Scientists say that within roughly 300,000 years, everything held within the singularity had expanded into a seething, opaque sphere of matter and radiation. As it did, the temperature dropped to 5,400 degrees Fahrenheit (3,000 degrees Celsius or 3273 Kelvin), allowing more stable particles to form. First, electrons and protons produced, which then combined to form hydrogen and helium atoms.

It means that the temperature dropped from 3273 Kelvin to about 3 Kelvin (today) in 15 billion years, see Figure (64) below:

Figure (64): Corresponding temperature of the universe expansion (exponential)

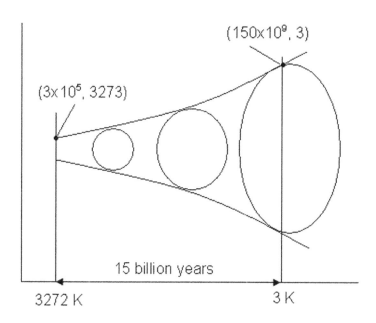

Solve for the two points (3x105, 3273), (150x109, 3), we have

$$AB^{3x\,10^5} + C = 3273$$

$$AB^{150x10^9} + C = 3$$

For simplicity consider C = 0

Now, we have two unknowns with two equations. Therefore, the values of A and B are as follows:

B = very small value (almost negligible)

A = very large value (almost infinity)

One can conclude that both temperatures must be the same value. This means either the expansion does not happen or the current temperature (3K) is not because of the cosmic microwave background (CMB) radiation.

Astronomers don't fully understand what caused the expansion to begin, but they use the term "Big Bang" to describe both the singularity and the first few moments that followed, in which the single point of super- dense material began to expand at an exponential rate.

The above solution was for the exponential rate. What about if the expansion was at a linear fashion, Figure (65)?

Figure (65): Corresponding temperature of the universe expansion (linear)

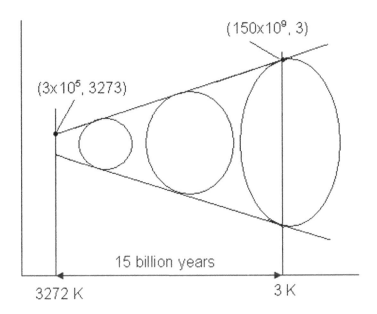

$(150x10^9, 3)$

$(3x10^5, 3273)$

15 billion years

3272 K

3 K

The slope formula is m = (Y2 –Y1)/(X1-X2) where m is the slope of the line AB, one can calculate the temperature before 300,000 years if the size of the universe is commensurable with the expansion, which is the case. The starting temperature would be 1011 K. This contradicts the temperature at 10-32 seconds after the Big Bang which is estimated at 1027 K.

34.2 Particle Cosmology and Quantum Cosmology Are More Speculative

Scientists suggested that the expansion of the universe comes from observation of the brightness of distant supernovae which is proportional to the redshift factor, which is (1+z), where z is the redshift. Assume the redshift factor is 1+z, then the slope of the expansion is 1 (tangent of the curve of the expansion, or the derivative of 1+z). If this is so, the universe is not closed; it is therefore an open universe. This could mean that the universe is of a flat type (Ω = 1), and its topology can be either compact or infinite. If it is compact, the expansion could be due to the dark energy. If it is infinite, the expansion could be due to something else (gravity is ruled out because it causes contraction to the universe). Maybe it was a result of a long-discarded version of Einstein's theory of gravity, one that contained what was called a "cosmological constant." Or maybe there was some strange kind of energy-fluid that filled space, or the vacuum is permeated by a "Higgs Field". If a Higgs field is excited, it would create forms of energy known as the "Higgs boson", which could interact with W and Z forces which may interact with the gravity to cause the expansion. No body knows.

The Chronology of the universe is illustrated in Figure (66). The right portion is the event in time and energy, and the left one is the slope of the expansion of the universe.

Figure (66): Time and energy versus the slope of expansion

Time, Second	Energy, eV	slope
4.7304E+17	0.003	-4.7E+17
1.26144E+13	1	-1.3E+07
1	1000000	-1E-09
1.00E-05	1.00E+09	-1E-16
1.00E-10	1.00E+11	-1E-35
1.00E-34	1.00E+25	-1E-63
1.00E-42	1.00E+29	1E-71

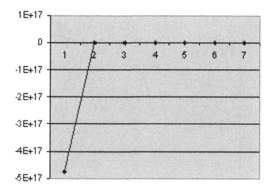

One can see the expansion from the Planck epoch (the highest energy) is very slow until the nucleosynthesis era when the Deuterium (heavy hydrogen), Helium and lithium are formed. The highest slope started only in our recent universe. This means that the maximum rate of expansion took place in our life on earth. In other worlds, the black energy (which is the main responsible factor for the expansion as it is believed) was greatly created just not long time ago. The question aroused is, was the gravity is responsible for the expansion?

Given that we do not have a fully self-consistent theory of the expansion, nor the quantum gravity, this makes the Big Bang theory and its three regimes of transitions (standard cosmology, particle cosmology and quantum cosmology) more speculative.

34.3 Redshift/ Blueshift and Expansion

Hubble's law describes the observation in physical cosmology that the velocity at which various galaxies and stars are receding from the earth is proportional to their distance from us. The recession velocity of the galaxies was inferred from their redshifts from the earth. Many were measured earlier by Vesto Slipher (1917) and related to velocity by him, Malcolm S Longair (2006). The Cosmic Century, Cambridge University Press. p.109. From Figure (67), one can deduce the following facts:

Figure (67): Redshift with respect to viewer 1 and viewer 2

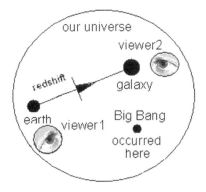

Viewer 1 observes the red shift, whereas viewer 2 observes the blueshift.

The galaxy in the figure leaves viewer 1 and comes closer to viewer 2.

The galaxy expands with respect to viewer 1 and contracts to viewer 2.

Because the location of the Big Bang is not known with respect to the universe, viewer 1 can judge that the universe is expanding and viewer 2 believes the universe is contracting.

The above conclusions can also be applied to the cosmic microwave background radiation (CMBR) if it is measured in a deep universe because the amplitude of the CMBR depends on galaxy properties which do change over space time, so precise measurement is impossible in the deep universe.

It is concluded that the precise model of the Big Bang theory is appealed from relatively far observations to the earth and from terrestrial laboratory experiments which incorporated into gravity and quantum physics.

34.4 Space Time and Expansion

Imagine a galaxy passing from point A to point B as shown in Figure (68).

Two observers are watching the galaxy at three different levels or distances.

Figure (68): observers see different distances and two different times

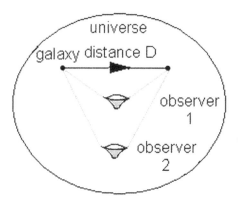

Observer 1 and observer 2 are watching the movement of the galaxy simultaneously. Observer 1 will see distance (D1) and observer 2 will see distance (D2) in a traveling time (T1) and (T2) respectively, assuming the galaxy travels at the speed of light and the distance between the two end points is measured in millions of light years. If this is true, the observer 1 will see the galaxy moving in a faster time than the observer 2. It means that an observer standing on the Earth will see the galaxy traveling in a different time than an observer standing on Sirius.

Now, if the general relativity does allow the space between distant objects to expand in such a way that the Hubble constant is 82/30.8 x1017 and the Hubble law is V = H0D, one can conclude:

Galaxies, including objects and particles, are traveling in different speeds that are not equal to the light speed.

The Hubble constant is valid for galaxies within a certain boundary.

The acceleration of galaxies, which depends on the traveling time, varies with respect to the observer's location.

The speed of the expansion varies, and therefore the rate of the expansion may be not 71 ± 4 (km/s)/Mpc, as derived from data collected by the WMAP satellite.

Imagine there are many observers in the universe watching the travel of galaxies; each observer will have his own calculations to find different rates of expansion. According to Davies (mathematical physicist Paul Davies, a professor at the University of Adelaide in Australia), if the rate of expansion at the moment of the Big Bang had differed by more than 10-18 seconds (one quintillionth of a second), there would have been no universe. Some scientists agreed to this calculation, but they emphasized that if there is a much larger difference in the rate of expansion of our recent universe, it would then collapse.

With respect to observer 1, the rate of expansion of the universe is increasing, and decreasing for observer 2.

In general, the Hubble law can not be verified because neither V nor D is directly observable, because they are properties of recent galaxies, whereas these parameters refer to the galaxies in the past, at the time that the light we currently see left it.

Although the Big Bang theory became accepted by a consensus of scientists, the ultimate fate of the universe became questionable. This depends upon the rate of expansion, the mass/energy and the density of the universe.

34.5 Space Time Created the Wormhole

Again consider Figure ( ) above in order to draw two different locations in a huge universe or in another worlds two universes. Figure (69) shows the wormhole.

Figure (69): Wormhole

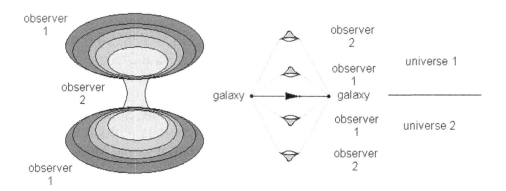

The worm hole is, in theory, much like a tunnel with two ends each in separate points in spacetime, and created due to negative energy density or negative gravity. Steve Hawkins believed that negative energy density existed in nature to stabilize the universe or universes. Inside this wormhole, our own universe was born. The wormhole was theorized to answer some of the most perplexing questions in cosmology, such as the Casimir effect. The Casimir effect is a small attractive or repulsive force that acts between two close parallel uncharged conducting plates. It is due to quantum vacuum fluctuations of the electromagnetic field. In fact, at separations of 10 nm between two plates—about 100 times the typical size of an atom—the Casimir effect produces the equivalent of 1 atmosphere of pressure (101.325 kPa), the precise value depending on surface geometry and other factors.

Scientists resort to the wormhole because they can not relate the gravity force to the three forces which are the weak force, the strong force and the electromagnetic force. Scientists are still puzzled by which force is responsible for the expansion. They came up with another idea that the dark energy could be the cause of the expansion. Theoretically, the expansion should still be slowing down; but to the contrary, the expansion is in fact accelerating. Some scientists theorize that an unknown force, called dark energy, may be the cause of this accelerated expansion, while others disagree. To satisfy those who disagree, scientists theorized the wormhole.

Scientists claim that the collapse of a giant star in another universe could have created a wormhole, a space-time conduit to another universe. Between these two openings, conditions could have developed that were similar to those we associate with the Big Bang, and our universe could have formed within the wormhole.

These conundrums may be a result of stopping the search for the riddle of the cosmos at the Big Bang, says Nikodem Poplawski of Indiana University in Bloomington.

If another universe existed near our universe, gravity could unite with other nuclear forces and electromagnetic forces in order to create the tunnel (conduit) between the two universes. The conduit bursts to cause the expansion of both universes. Therefore, the wormhole could be accounted for our expanding universe – rather than the elusive dark energy. Do you believe that?

35. Conclusion

The so called "Big Crunch" model that followed the "Big Bang" model may not be the end of the universe as scientists suggested. The cycle between the two models repeats it self for infinity with the possibility of an oscillating universe along the path of the cycle. These two models have ancient parallels, both in the Hindu and ancient Greece, and in few other faiths.

The Hindu tradition perceives the existence of the cyclical nature of the universe and everything within it. Hindus believes in nothingness (singularity) as the start point of the Big Bang.

In the beginning there was neither existence nor non- existence; there was no atmosphere, no sky, and no realm beyond the sky. What power was there? Where was that power? Who was that power? Was it finite or infinite?

There was neither death nor immortality. There was nothing to distinguish night from day. There was no wind or breath. God alone breathed by his own energy. Other than God there was nothing.
In the beginning darkness was swathed in darkness. All was liquid and formless. God was clothed in emptiness.

The question is did scientists such as Georges Lemaître, Stephen Hawkins and others steal the idea of the Big Bing (with its basic singularity point) from Hindu or ancient Greece?

The Big Bang theory cannot be proved by experiment, as it operates on too large a scale. It is like Darwinian evolution which can only be inferred by extrapolation. One can not use the analogy of explosions of nuclear atomic bomb with a dimensionless huge space such as our universe. The bomb explosion and the Big Bang are two different to compare.

Our mind can not conceptualize the idea saying that in the beginning there was nothing… and from that nothing came a Big Bang, caused by no one coming from nowhere… It created all the mass of the universe completely by chance [according to Einstein's Theory]…

Good mathematicians can solve complicated equations when they provide the principles of hypotheses to the equations. For example, you can assume the velocity vs. redshift movement faster than light if you work in a frame beyond the special relativity as suggested by Einstein. Therefore, a variety of possible shapes of a galaxy can be inferred if you work in different relativities, say, the general relativity.

Even if you work in the general relativity, one scientist may consider the effect of gravity, and the conclusion is contraction of the universe until it reached the Big Crunch. So, three different models can be established from three different scientists. In other words, the universe expands exponentially with different relativity, inflates at special relativity, or contracts if it subjected to a dark matter (gravity). Mr. Hubble will then be confused as to where he will use his constant.

Because of this, the idea of the Big Bang and the Big Crunch has never been popular in modern scientific cosmology.

The purpose of the Big Bang theory is to construct a philosophy allowing people to live debauched and pleasure-seeking lives confident that, "There is no God, there is no life after death, the universe was created by chance". Most people will be happy if there is no restriction on chasing women, fame, profit, adoration and distinction, but only a few are interested in spiritual life. The brainwashed general publics are prepared to believe such nonsense when presented by the scientists – the mathematicians. The Big Bang is a tenable theory as long as the idea of "soul" is present: that the conscious impulse is driving everything even towards opposite things. Also tenable theories created by real scientists may be obsolete tomorrow after they accepted such theories as valid theories.

The scientific achievement that is related to the industrial revolution marks a major turning point in human history; almost every aspect of daily life was eventually influenced in some way. Most notably, average income and population began to exhibit unprecedented sustained growth. Due to this, Christianity declined in influence in many western countries, in Western Europe and elsewhere. Secularism (separating religion from politics and science) increased in the 20th century.

That is why science, in its purest form, is very influential and will never weigh in on God, because scientists always take the attitude called the Burden of Proof towards God (or shame), saying that God, for their purposes, does not exist until proved physically. While this is a healthy attitude to take towards matters physical, their mental approach is still towards theism, and they are quite vocally so and have gotten to the point where they would disbelieve God even if they saw physical proof for Him. This is what you talk about when you mention scientists' "blind faith," and it must be avoided, both in science and in religion.

Two leading scientists (Newton and Einstein) took control of our mind. Imagine two amateur persons listening to an argument between Newton and Einstein discussing the effect of gravity and the relativity on the universe. Newton said the curvature of an object (rotation of a planet) is because it is rotating with respect to the distant stars, or in other words, in classical physics, an inertial reference frame is one in which an object that experiences no forces does not accelerate. Meanwhile, Einstein responded to negate Newton's claim by saying that an object standing on the earth, however, will experience a force, as it is being held against the geodesic by the surface of the planet. In light of this, the planet rotating in empty space will experience a force because it rotates with respect to the geodesic sapcetime. They will take a shape of a ball, not because it is rotating with respect to the distant star (say the sun), but because it is rotating with respect to the geodesic.

Some of the amateur persons who listen to both Newton and Einstein will either agree with Newton or Einstein, and some don't understand what they are talking about. But all persons will pay respect to both scientists and will be brainwashed by them. Probably they believed a lie that conflicted with the truth previously given to them.

Brainwashing can extend to groups of people without a limit in size or scope. Millions of people were brainwashed to believe the Big Bang was the best theory of the creation of the universe until the recent discovery of very distant galaxies that must have already been tens of billions of years old at the time whereas the Big Bang is said to have 13.75 billion years. The biggest proof of this is the UDFy-38135539 which is the Hubble Ultra Deep Field (UDF) classification for a galaxy which has been calculated (as of October 2010 [update]) to have a light travel time of 13 billion years with a present commoving distance of around 30 billion light years. The galaxy is thus the most distant object in the universe yet to have been observed.

The quantum theory does not explain the discrete intervals at which the red shifts fall. Even Mr. Hubble does not take the relative velocity of the red shifts into his account. This means that the assumption that the expansion of the universe is based on the red shift must be abandoned. Even if the red shifts are based on a quantized velocity, this infers that the universe is expanding intermittently, in an on-off pattern, or in a cyclic motion. If it is so, what is the force behind such an intermittent/oscillating expansion?

The other possibility, if the red shifts are falling in discrete function, is that the universe is not expanding which means there was no moment of creation and no Big Bang.

Scientists can not explain why the greatest black holes of all don't behave like a black hole. Scientists wonder if there were there different sizes of stellar coming out from one singular point, different sizes of quarks and liptons to create different stars and galaxies, or different Bosons. If it is so, this will invalidate the quantum physics and Bose-Einstein statistics. Cosmologists promoted the Big Bang theory in different periods: the first period of "rulelessness" for about 3 seconds, the second period of light (semi-ruleness), and the third period of the formation of the galaxies (ruleness). Scientists talked about the last two periods, for example, Einstein talked about the second period, Newton talked about the third period, Hubble talked about the second period and some of the first period, but no body could touch the first period. Scientists enjoyed talking about periods where the gravity and quantum physics could not be applied in the first period. Then who can talk about the first period? Is he the God we know or some people with autism?

Although both scientists are believed to have autism (researchers at Cambridge and Oxford universities believe both scientists displayed signs of Asperger's Syndrome (an autism spectrum disorder) [http://news.bbc.co.uk/2/hi/health/2988647.stm]), they could not go before the second period.

Walter Baade, a German birth, discovered that the stars in our Galaxy can be divided into two basic groups: Population I and Population II. Population I stars have a greater abundance of elements heavier than helium than the Population II stars which were immediately formed after the Big Bang. Stellar populations are categorized as I, and II, with each group having decreasing metal content and increasing age.

The question is was it fusion or fission during the Big Bang? If it was fusion, there should be a mass somewhere to create such huge energy and temperature (temperature was 1027 C o at 10-32 seconds). The huge energy then converted to a mass of hydrogen which in turns was converted to helium, carbon and finally oxygen. The huge energy at the start of the Big Bang should be able to create massive and heavy objects from the formula $E = MC2$. Therefore, Population II stars should have heavy metal contents. If it was fission that was involved in splitting the nucleus of an atom, this yielded two or more lighter nuclei and a large amount of energy. This means that large atoms converted to small atoms, or in other world, helium converted to hydrogen, which is the reversed process of the Big Bang theory.

Cosmologists claimed that Dark ages occurred after 380,000 years after the Big Bang. The cosmic microwave background (CMB) was then created from the period 380,000 years up to and including the time that first stars (galaxy) had formed, which was estimated about 400 million years. The stars then emitted photons to ionize hydrogen to protons and electrons, of which the process is called 'decoupling'. As per the Hubble telescope, the reading of the red shift (z) was 1100, which corresponds to the infrared spectrum of 2.2 μm, which is close to the visible light spectrum. This means that the period is not a dark period, and far from the peak CMB recorded (2mm). This would have three conclusions:

There was no decoupling of the hydrogen to convert to helium.

The Dark Age could be much before 380,000years. It could have happened before the decoupling of ions and electrons epoch (10-30 seconds).

The CMB occurred after the creation of the first stars and galaxies.

Until this point in time, we don't have an idea of just when the Dark age, CMB and hydrogen conversion to helium started, or how long the process took.

A Perspective on the Relation of Science and Religion

Psychology's previously negative response (represented by psychologists such as Durkhiem, Weber, Freud, Malinowski and others) towards religion was premised on outdated understandings of science and an overly narrow professionalism. Contemporary philosophy of science breaks down the radical demarcation between science and religion. Religion and science are different, but they cannot be categorically separated or viewed as mutually exclusive. A proposal is developed for how religion could participate as an active partner with psychology as a science and as an applied professional discipline.

William Bragg quoted (Noble prize in physics): "Religion and science are opposed...but only in the same sense as that in which my thumb and forefinger are opposed - and between the two, one can grasp everything." He also said "The important thing in science is not so much to obtain new facts as to discover new ways of thinking about them."

36. Wrapping Up

The philosophy of the creation of the universe from the singularity (nothingness) point until the present universe, which was formulated among the Hindus and the ancient Greeks, has also been repeated from time to time in some cultures and has been developed temperamentally. It falsely holds that the universe has always been created by coincidence and was not created by supernatural being. Those philosophers who believe in coincidental creation of the universe still believe that babies who are created from nothingness are created by a supernatural being.

Theistic evolutionists believe that there is a God that God is the creator of the material universe and (by consequence) all life within, and that biological evolution is simply a natural process within that creation. Evolution, according to this view, is simply a tool that God employed to develop human life.

An interview with scientists by BBC showed that most natural scientists (astronomy, biology, chemistry, earth science, and physics), believe in creationism (the belief that God created the universe). Some natural scientists also believe in traducianism, which means that the immaterial aspect is transmitted through natural generation along with the body. The material aspect of human beings; in other words, an individual's soul is derived from the souls of the individual's parents. On the contrary, statistics showed that scientists of humanities (philosophy, literature, and art, that are concerned with human thought and culture; the liberal arts) believe in coincidental creation. In general, a 1995 survey attributed to the Encyclopedia Britannica indicates that the non-religious are about 14.7% of the world's population, and atheists around 3.8%. Another survey attributed to Britannica shows the population of atheists at around 2.4% of the world's population.

The principle of creation of both human and universe is still the same; both are created from nothingness. The theory of evolution of human, widely referred to as Darwinism, is another claim and belief in coincidence.

In the 20th century, an important change took place in the science that many scientists were faithful people who were in agreement that the universe was created not coincidentally, but by God. However, because of politics, economy, social conditions and materialism, the philosophy of coincidental creationists gained wide acceptance and spread throughout the developed world.

It should be noted that despite American society being secular and atheist in theory, 76.5% of Americans seem to call themselves Christian, thus American public society underrepresents and in many cases completely disenfranchises the implementation of the majority opinion: that there is a God. In this sense, 14.1% of American societies which call themselves secularists decide policy, scientific opinion, educational course material, and many other forms of knowledge despite the fact the majority of American society believes in a higher power of some sort, [http://www.nwcreation.net/atheism.html].

Here are some quotations by prominent scientists and people.

Sir Ernest Chain, Co-holder of the 1945 Noble Prize for developing penicillin
"To postulate that the development and survival of the fittest is entirely a consequence of chance mutation seems to me a hypothesis based on no evidence and irreconcilable with the facts."
These classical evolutionary theories are a gross over-simplification of an immensely complex and intricate mass of facts, and it amazes me that they are swallowed so uncritically and readily, and for such a long time, by so many scientists without a murmur of protest."
..."I would rather believe in fairy tales than in such wild speculation. I have said for years that speculations about the origin of life lead to no useful purpose as even the simplest living system is far too complex to be understood in terms of the extremely primitive chemistry scientists have used in their attempts to explain the unexplainable. God cannot be explained away by such naive thoughts."
Quoted by Ronald W. Clark, the Life of Ernst Chain (London: Weidenfield & Nicolson, 1985), pp. 147-148

Subrahmanyan Chandrasekhar (Noble Prize winner in physics) – "In fact, I consider myself an atheist. But I have a feeling of disappointment because the hope for contentment and a peaceful outlook on life as the result of pursuing a goal has remained largely unfulfilled. What? I don't understand. You mean, single–minded pursuit of science, understanding parts of nature and comprehending nature with such enormous success still leaves you with a feeling of discontentment? I don't really have a sense of fulfillment. All I have done seems to not be very much".

Michael Polyani (Professor of chemistry and then philosophy at the University of Manchester. His son, John Polyani, won the Nobel prize) – "I shall reexamine the suppositions underlying our belief in science and propose to show that they are more extensive than is usually thought. They will appear to coextend with the entire spiritual foundations of man and to go to the very root of his social existence. Hence I will urge our belief in science should be regarded as a token of much wider convictions".

Francis Bacon (an English scientist and philosopher) – "Let no one think or maintain that a person can search too far or be too well studied in either the book of God's word or the book of God's works. They that deny a God destroy man's nobility; for certainly man is of kin to the beasts in his body; and, if he be not of kin to God by his spirit, he is a base and ignoble creature".

Blaise Pascal (French mathematician, physicist and inventor) – "God makes people conscious of their inward wretchedness, which the Bible calls "sin" and his infinite mercy. He unites himself to their inmost soul, fills it with humility and joy, with confidence and love, renders them incapable of any other end than Himself. Jesus Christ is the end of all and the centre to which all tends". He said, "God of Abraham, God of Isaac, God of Jacob, not of the philosophers and the scholars…" and concluded by quoting Psalm 119:16: "I will not forget thy word. Amen." He seems to have carefully sewn this document into his coat and always transferred it when he changed clothes.

Sir Isaac Newton (an English physicist, mathematician and astronomer) –"This most beautiful system of the sun, planets and comets could only proceed from the counsel and dominion of an intelligent and powerful Being". He said, "Gravity explains the motions of the planets, but it cannot explain who set the planets in motion. God governs all things and knows all that is or can be done." He said "He (God) is eternal and infinite, omnipotent and omniscient; that is, his duration reaches from eternity to eternity; his presence from infinity to infinity; he governs all things, and knows all things that are or can be done. …We know him only by his most wise and excellent contrivances of things... [W]e revere and adore him as his servants"

Michael Faraday (an English physicist and chemist who contributed to the field of electromagnetism and electrochemistry) had the courage to turn down a government request that he develop poison gases for use in the Crimean War. He refused to buy insurance, believing that to do so was to show lack of faith... He believed the universe is intelligible, beautiful, and adaptable to man's use designed by a rational, wise, and good God. Faraday was close to death. A friend and well–wisher came by and said, "Sir Michael, what speculations have you now?" Faraday answered: Speculations, man, I have none. I have certainties. I thank God that I don't rest my dying head upon speculations for "I know whom I have believed and am persuaded that he is able to keep that which I've committed unto him against that day".

John Clerk Maxwell (a Scottish theoretical physicist and mathematician) – "Think what God has determined to do to all those who submit themselves to his righteousness and are willing to receive his gift [of eternal life in Jesus Christ]. They are to be conformed to the image of his Son and when that is fulfilled and God sees they are conformed to the image of Christ, there can be no more condemnation".

William Thompson (a Scottish mathematician and physicist who contributed to many branches of physics) – "Do not be afraid to be free thinkers. If you think strongly enough, you will be forced by science to the belief in God".

Joseph John Thomson (a British Physicist and noble prize winner. He is the discoverer of the electron and isotopees and the inventor of the mass spectrometer) – "In the distance tower still higher [scientific] peaks which will yield to those who ascend them still wider prospects and deepen the feeling whose truth is emphasized by every advance in science, that great are the works of the Lord".

Charles Coulson (a British scientist in mathematics, physics, chemistry, and molecular biology) probably would have received the Nobel but he died before the age of 65 which was the condition for the Noble prize test at that time. Coulson testified "There were some ten of us and together we sought for God and together we found Him. I learned for the first time in my life that God was my friend. God became real to me, utterly real. I knew Him and could talk with Him as I never imagined it before and these prayers were the most glorious moment of the day. Life had a purpose and that purpose coloured everything".

Louis Pasteur (a French chemist and microbiologist. He discovered the first vaccine for rabies and anthrax) – "A bit of science distances one from God, but much science nears one to him".

Wernher von Braun (NASA director and father of the American Space Program) – "There simply cannot be a creation without some kind of Spiritual Creator...in the world around us we can behold the obvious manifestation of the Divine plan of the Creator".

William Daniel Phillips (an American physicist and shered the Noble Prize in physics for 1997 with Steven Chu and Claude Cohen-Tannoudji) – "Being an ordinary scientist and an ordinary Christian seems perfectly natural to me." He also said, "I'm strongly of the conviction that God is personal, and this is the foundation of my faith".

J.Y. Chen (a Chinese Paleontologist) – "In China its O.K. to criticize Darwin but not the government, while in the United States its O.K. to criticize the government, but not Darwin".

George Wald (an American biochemist and Noble laureate in medicine) – "When it comes to the origin of life on this earth, there are only two possibilities: creation or spontaneous generation (evolution). There is no third way. Spontaneous generation was disproved 100 years ago, but that leads us only to one other conclusion: that of supernatural creation. We cannot accept that on philosophical grounds (personal reasons); therefore we choose to believe the impossible:that life arose spontaneously by chance".

Colin Patterson (an English senior palaeontologist, British Museum of Natural History, London) –"The question is: Can you tell me anything you know about Evolution? Any one thing? Any one thing that is true? I tried that question on the geology staff at the Field Museum of Natural History and the only answer I got was silence. I tried it on the members of the Evolutionary Morphology Seminar in the University of Chicago, a very prestigious body of Evolutionists, and all I got there was silence for a long time, and eventually one person said, "I do know one thing - it ought not to be taught in high school".

Akbar S Ahmed (currently the Ibn Khaldun Chair of Islamic Studies, American University in Washington D.C., the First Distinguished Chair of Middle East and Islamic Studies at the US Naval Academy, Annapolis, and a Nonresident Senior Fellow at the Brookings Institution. He is considered "the world's leading authority on contemporary Islam" by the BBC) – "God is the source of all creation and disposer of all lives and events".

Mohammad Abdus Salam (a Pakistani theoretical physicist, astrophysicist and Noble laureate in physics for his work in Electro-Weak Theory) – "The Holy Quran enjoins us to reflect on the verities of Allah's created laws of nature; however, that our generation has been privileged to glimpse a part of His design is a bounty and a grace for which I render thanks with a humble heart". [Abdus Salam Nobel Prize in Physics Biography]

Harun Yahia (a Turkish proponent of Islamic creationism. He supports the Old Earth creationism) – "The expansion of the universe is one of the most important pieces of evidence that the universe was created out of nothing. Although this was not discovered by science until the 20th century, Allah has informed us of this reality in the Qur'an revealed 1,400 years ago:
It is We Who have built the universe with (Our creative) power, and, verily, it is We Who are steadily expanding it. (Surat adh-Dhariyat: 47)".

John L. Esposito (a professor of International Affairs and Islamic Studies at Georgetown University. He is also the director of the Prince Alwaleed Bin Talal center for Muslim-Christian understanding at Georgetown University) – "And science will return to its authentic and true paradigm: A search for the discovery and definition of the great design and harmony in the natural world, the artifact of God".

The book of Muslims (the Quran) said "The science of modern cosmology, observational and theoretical, clearly indicates that, at one point in time, the whole universe was nothing but a cloud of "smoke."

"Allah is talking about human being in an honoring way and puts humanity in light. Human being is made aware about the things that are both seen and those that is beyond human perception. All the scientific inventions such as the use of satellites, cell phones etc. are due to the fact that human beings are made aware about these things."[C:\Documents and Settings\Amin\Desktop\Humanity in the Quran.mht].
Do ye not see that Allah has subjected to your (use) all things in the heavens and on earth, and has made his bounties flow to you in exceeding measure, (both) seen and unseen? Yet there are among men those who dispute about Allah, without knowledge and without guidance, and without a Book to enlighten them! (Quran 31:20)

Glossaries and Illustrations

Acceleration – a change in motion = (the velocity change)/(time interval of change). It involves a change in the speed (increase or decrease) OR direction OR both speed and direction.

Accretion disk – a disk of gas that forms around a massive object as material spirals onto the massive object. Accretion disks around white dwarfs, neuron stars, and black holes, are formed form when material is drawn off a nearby normal or giant star. Accretion disks around neuron stars and black holes can be hot enough to radiate X-rays.

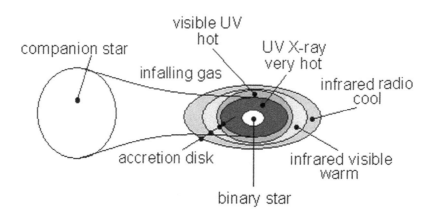

Active galaxy – luminous galaxy that produces most of its energy from a very compact source at its center. It has a non-thermal continuous spectrum. The energy is coming from an accretion disk of gas around a supermassive black hole at the nucleus of the galaxy.

Albedo – the fraction of light reflected from an object. Specified as a decimal fraction from 0 (total absorption) to 1 (total reflection).

Altitude – a position on the celestial sphere that is the number of degrees an object is above the nearest horizon. It varies from 0° at horizon to 90° at zenith which is the vertical position of an object.

Angular momentum – a measure of the amount of spin or orbital motion an object has. It is proportional to the mass of the object multiplied by its radius multiplied by its spin or orbital speed.

Annular eclipse – a type of solar eclipse that happens when the sun and Moon are exactly lined up but the Moon is too far away from the earth to totally block the Sun's surface. A ring (annulus) of sunlight is seen around the dark Moon (contrast with total solar eclipse).

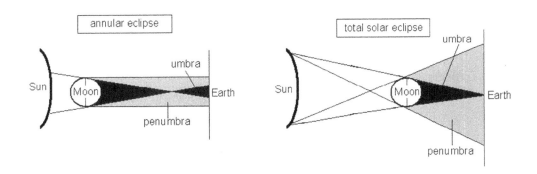

Aphelion – point in an object's orbit around the sun that is furthest from the Sun.

Apparent magnitude – the apparent brightness of an object measured by an observer at an arbitrary distance away.

Asteroid – boulder to mountain-sized piece of rock remaining from the early solar system. The largest asteroid is only 1000 kilometers across but most are much smaller.

Astrology – a non-scientific belief system in which the positions of the planets among the stars are thought to hold the key to understanding what you can expect from life.

Astronomical unit (AU) – average distance between the Earth and the Sun (149.6 million kilometers). Used for interplanetary distances.

Astronomy – a discipline that uses the scientific method to understand the physical universe (usually beyond the Earth's atmosphere).

Astrophysics – a branch of astronomy that deals with the physical properties and interactions of celestial bodies---the application of the principles of physics to celestial bodies and phenomena.

Aurora australis – aurorae seen in the southern hemisphere.

Aurora borealis – aurorae seen in the northern hemisphere.

Aurorae – light displays produced by molecules and atoms high up in an atmosphere. The gas particles are excited by collisions with solar wind particles that were deflected by the planet's magnetic field toward the magnetic poles of the planet.

Autumnal equinox – specific moment in the year (on September 22) when the Sun is directly on the celestial equator, moving south of the celestial equator.

Azimuth – position on the celestial sphere that is the number of degrees along the horizon away from the exact north point. Exact North = 0°, exact East = 90°, exact South = 180°, exact West = 270°, exact North = 360° (or 0°). It is a horizontal position of an object.

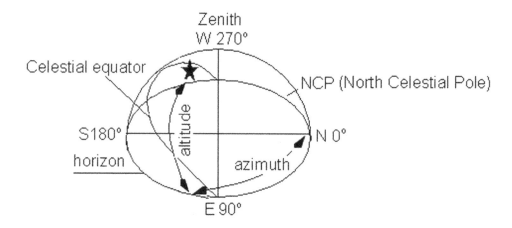

Big Bang – a theory of the creation of the universe from an ultra-compact volume with very high temperatures about 13.7 billion years ago. The ultra-compact volume began expanding and is responsible for the expanding motion we see today.

Black hole – a collapsed core for the most massive stars, formed from the total collapse of a core greater than 3 solar masses to an infinitesimal point of infinite density. Gravity in the region surrounding the collapsed core is so strong that the escape velocity is greater than the speed of light. Far beyond that region, black holes obey Newton's law of gravity.

Blueshift – spectral lines are shifted from an object to shorter wavelengths because the object is moving toward the observer. The greater the speed of the object, the greater the blueshift will be.

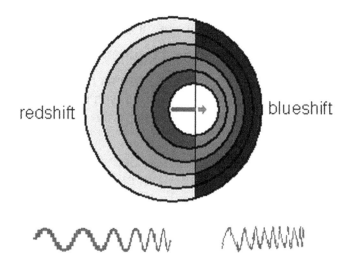

Brown dwarf – object formed from the gravitational collapse of a gas cloud just as a star is but having too little mass (less than 0.08 solar masses) to undergo nuclear fusion reactions.

Carbonaceous meteorite – a type of stone meteorite containing silicates, carbon compounds (giving them their dark color), around 20% water, and sometimes amino acids (the building blocks of proteins used in biological processes of life).

Celestial equator – a great circle that is a projection of the Earth's equator onto the sky. Always intercepts horizon at exact East and exact West point. Its meridian altitude = (90 degrees - observer's latitude). We see one-half of its circle at a time (12 hours worth).

Celestial sphere – an imaginary sphere of extremely large size around the Earth on which the stars appear to be placed.

Center of mass – the balance point between two massive objects that is proportionally closer to the more massive object. It is the point where (mass object 1) × (object 1 distance from center of mass) = (mass object 2) × (object 2 distance from center of mass).

Centripetal force – a force directed inward.

Cepheid – a type of variable star that changes brightness by changing size and temperature with a period that depends on its average luminosity. More luminous Cepheids have longer pulsation periods. Cepheids are particularly valuable for determining distances to the nearby galaxies in which they reside. Distances to Cepheids are derived from measurements of their pulsation periods and apparent brightnesses and application of the inverse square law of light brightness.

Chondrule – round glassy structure 0.5 to 5 millimeters in diameter embedded in a primitive stone meteorite. It is a solidified droplet of matter from the early solar nebula and is the very oldest part of the primitive meteorite.

Circumpolar – when an object is close enough to either the north celestial pole or south celestial pole (within an angular distance = observer's latitude) such that the object never moves below an observer's horizon or never rises above the horizon as the Earth rotates.

Closed universe – a universe with enough matter (gravity) to eventually stop the expansion and recollapse (it has a "closed future").

Coma (comet) – large atmosphere around a comet's nucleus that forms when the nucleus nears the Sun and warms up (usually at around Saturn's or Uranus' distance from the Sun).

Coriolis Effect – the deflection sideways of an object moving across the surface of a rotating body caused by the rotation of the body. The coriolis effect makes storms spiral on the Earth and produces the banded cloud layers on the gas giant planets.

Corona – the top layer of the Sun's atmosphere. It is up to a few million degrees in temperature, but has very low density so the amount of heat is small. It is the pearly-white "crown" or glow seen around the dark Moon during a total solar eclipse.

Cosmic microwave background radiation – it is a radio microwave energy that is nearly uniform in all directions and has a nearly perfect thermal spectrum. It is the greatly redshifted remnant of the early hot universe produced about 380,000 years after the birth of the universe.

Cosmic rays – extremely high-energy (very fast-moving) sub-atomic particles, mostly protons, in space. Some produced by the Sun. Others produced in star deaths such as supernovae. Highest energy cosmic rays are of unknown origin.

Cosmological constant – an extra term Albert Einstein put in his equations of General Relativity that would act as a repulsive form of gravity to balance the attractive nature of gravity and keep the universe static. Einstein abandoned the concept after the observation of the Hubble redshift indicated that the universe might not be stationary

Cosmological principle – an assumption that the universe is everywhere uniform and looks the same in any direction---it is homogeneous and isotropic.

Cosmology – the study of the nature and origin of the universe and how it changes over time.

Critical density – boundary density between enough mass/volume to eventually stop the expansion of the universe and too little mass/volume to eventually stop the expansion.

Dark energy – an additional energy needed to make the universe's overall curvature flat. It may be the cosmological constant.

Dark matter – material that does not emit any light (or not detected yet), but has a significant gravitational effect.

Declination – position on the celestial sphere that is the number of degrees an object is north or south of the celestial equator. It is a projection of latitude lines onto the sky. An object's declination is fixed with respect to the stars. Varies from --90° at the SCP to 0° at the celestial equator to +90° at the NCP. It is a vertical position of an object.

Deuterium – an isotope of hydrogen with one proton and one neutron in the nucleus.

Doppler Effect – an apparent change in the wavelength of energy produced by an object that is caused by the object's motion towards or away from the observer (along the line of sight). In astronomical spectra, the Doppler Effect is seen in the shifting of spectral lines.

Doppler shift technique (planet detection) – a method of finding exoplanets by looking for a periodic alternating redshift and blueshift of a star.

Dust – one component of the interstellar medium that is made of thin, highly flattened flakes or needles of graphite and silicates coated with water ice and other frozen gases. It is responsible for the reddening and extinction of starlight.

Dust tail (comet) – one of the two tails of a comet made of dust grains that curve away from the Sun from the action of the photons in the sunlight pushing the dust grains away from Sun. It has a yellow-white color from reflected sunlight.

Drake Equation – an equation that estimates the number of communicating advanced civilizations inhabiting the Galaxy.

Eclipsing binary – two stars orbiting each other in a plane that is along your line of sight so you see one star periodically pass in front of the other star. They are especially useful for determining the diameters and masses of stars.

Ecliptic – great circle that is a projection of the Earth's orbit onto the sky, or the path the Sun takes through the stars in its annual motion. It is tilted by 23.5° with respect to the celestial equator.

Electromagnetic radiation – a form of energy made of oscillating electric and magnetic fields. It is a fancy word for light' and it includes (in order of increasing energy) radio, infrared, visible light (optical), ultraviolet, X-rays, and gamma rays.

Electron – negatively-charged subatomic particle that moves around the atomic nucleus in specific energy levels. It has about 1800 times less mass than the proton and neutron.

Electron degeneracy pressure – pressure exerted by a degenerate gas made of electrons. It is what prevents further collapse of a white dwarf.

Element – a substance that cannot be decomposed by chemical means into simpler substances. All atoms of an element have the same number of protons in the nucleus.

Ellipse – squashed circle that tapers at both ends. The total of the distance between any point on the ellipse and one focus + the distance from the point to the other focus = a constant. It is the shape of bound orbits.

Elliptical galaxy – a galaxy with a smooth, rounded appearance. Early large burst of star formation long ago used up all of their original gas and dust. Star orbits are aligned in more random directions and have greater eccentricities than star orbits in spiral galaxies.

Emission line spectrum – bright lines in a spectrum that are produced by hot, thin (low-pressure) gases. Made by electrons jumping down closer to the nucleus of the atom.

Epicycle – a device in Ptolemy's Earth-centered model that makes a planet execute a small circular motion around a point that is itself in a circular orbit around the Earth. It was used to explain retrograde motion.

Equation of state – the relation that describes the state or condition of a material as determined by how the temperature, density, and pressure depend on each other in the material.

Equation of Time – a relation that describes the difference in time between the meridian crossings of the mean sun and the actual Sun.

Equinox - point on the sky where the ecliptic and the celestial equator intercept. When the Sun is at the equinox point, it is on the celestial equator and we have 12 hours of daylight. Vernal (spring) equinox: March 21; autumnal equinox: September 22.

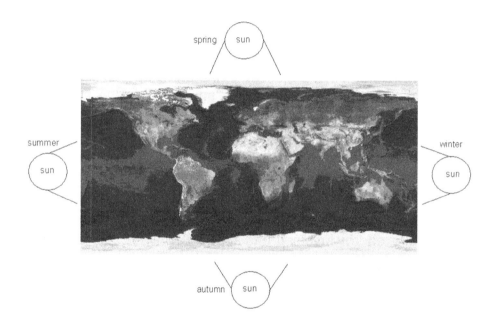

Erosion – the breaking down or building up of geological structures and transporting of material by ice, liquid, or wind.

Escape velocity – the initial speed an object needs to escape a massive body's gravitational influence and never return.

Event horizon – the distance from a black hole's center at which the escape velocity equals the speed of light. No information of events occurring inside the event horizon can get to the outside.

Exoplanet – a planet orbiting another star (other than our Sun) beyond our solar system.

Exosphere – uppermost layer a planet's atmosphere where the gases escape to space. Very low density gases heated by X-rays and ultraviolet light.

Extinction – reduction in the intensity of the light (the number of photons) from a celestial body as the light passes through a dust cloud. Dust clouds in space make stars behind the dust clouds appear dimmer than they would be if the dust was not there.

Flat universe – a universe that stop expanding only after an infinite amount of time (a special case of an open universe).

Galactic cannibalism – the swallowing up whole of a small galaxy by a large galaxy (usually a large elliptical galaxy at the center of a galaxy cluster).

Galaxy – a very large cluster of stars (tens of millions to trillions of stars) gravitationally bound together.

General Relativity – a theory invented by Albert Einstein to describe gravity. It says that gravity is a warping or distortion of spacetime around a massive object. Although it applies everywhere in the universe, General Relativity must be used instead of Newton's law of gravity in regions of strong gravity.

Geocentric (universe) – model of the universe with the Earth at the center and all other objects moving around it.

Giant impact theory – explanation about how the Moon was formed from mantle material blown out by the impact of a Mars-sized (or larger) planet with the Earth several billion years ago. The ejected material condensed to form the Moon.

Giant molecular cloud – large, dense gas cloud (with some dust) that is cold enough for molecules to form. A typical giant molecular cloud has a few hundred thousand to a few million solar masses of material. Stars form in them.

Globular cluster – spherical cluster of hundreds of thousands to millions of very old stars. The orbits of most globular clusters are very elliptical and oriented in random directions.

Granulation – bright spots of convection on the Sun's surface 700 to 1000 kilometers across forming a honeycomb pattern. Formed from hot, bright gas rising from below in the center of a granule and cooler, dimmer gas falling back down at the edge of a granule.

Gravitational lens – the focusing of light from a distant object by the warped space-time around a massive body (such as a galaxy) between you and the distant object as predicted by General Relativity.

Gravitational redshift – the lengthening of the wavelength of electromagnetic radiation as it moves away from a region of intense gravity.

Gravity – a fundamental force of nature between two objects that is proportional to the product of their masses and inversely proportional to the square of the distance between their respective centers. It depends on nothing else.

Greenhouse effect – the trapping of heat energy close to a planet's surface by certain types of gases in the atmosphere (e.g., water, methane, and carbon dioxide). These gases allow visible light from the Sun to reach the surface but prevent the infrared light from the heated surface to radiate back to space.

Ground state – the lowest energy state of an atom---all of the electrons are as close to the nucleus as possible.

H II region – cloud of ionized hydrogen around a hot, luminous star (usually O or B-type). Produced by the copious ultraviolet light from the hot star(s) causing the hydrogen to fluoresce (atoms are ionized and then when the electron recombine, they produce energy in the visible band).

Half-life – the time required for one-half of a radioactive material to decay to a more stable material (it is NOT one-half the age of the rock!).

Heliocentric (universe) – model of the universe with the Sun at the center and all other objects moving around it.

Helioseismology – the study of the Sun's interior from observations of the Sun's pulsations on its surface.

Helium flash – in low-mass red giant stars, the onset of the fusing of helium in the core can be very rapid, almost explosive.

Hubble constant – slope of the line relating the speed of the galaxies away from each other and their distance apart from each other.

Hubble Law – the relationship between a galaxy's recession speed from other galaxies and the distance between them: the recession speed = H × distance, where H is the Hubble constant. The recession speed is derived from the redshift of the galaxy spectra and with the Hubble Law; it can be used to find the distance to the farthest galaxies.

Inertia – the property of an object describing its tendency to stay at the same velocity (or at rest) unless a force acts on it.

Inflation – a brief period of ultra-rapid expansion in the very early universe about 10-38 to 10-36 seconds after the Big Bang.

Irregular galaxy – a galaxy with no definite structure. Stars are distributed in bunches placed randomly throughout the galaxy. Many irregular galaxies have a lot of gas and dust still left in them from which stars are now forming.

Isotope – a sub-group of an element in which the atomic nucleus has the same number of neutrons, as well as, the same number of protons. All of the atoms of an element will have very nearly the same chemical properties, but the isotopes can have very different nuclear properties.

Kepler's 1st law – orbits are ellipses with the central object at one focus (not the center!). There is nothing at the other focus.

Kepler's 2nd law – a line between the satellite and the central object sweeps out equal areas in equal intervals of time. A satellite moves faster when it is closer to the massive body it orbits and moves slower when farther from the massive object.

Kepler's 3rd law – for an object in an elliptical orbit around a massive body, the square of the orbital period is proportional to the cube of the average distance of the orbiting object from the massive body. The massive body's mass is proportional to the (average distance)3/(orbital period)2. In general, for two objects orbiting a common point between them, their combined mass is proportional to: (average distance between them)3/(their orbital period)2.

Kuiper Belt – a disk of comets beyond Neptune's orbit (or 30 to 100+ A.U.) that orbit roughly in the same plane as the planets. Many of the short period comets come from the Kuiper Belt.

Latitude – used to specify position on the Earth, it is the number of degrees north or south of the Earth's equator.

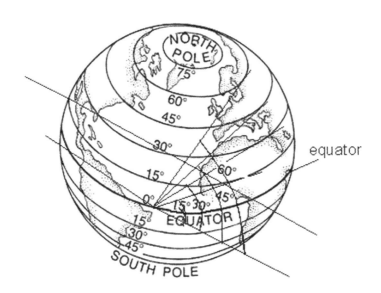

Law of gravity (Newton's) – the force of mutual attraction between two objects = mass 1 × mass 2 / (distance between the objects)2. The term G is a universal constant of nature that always = 6.672× 10-11 meter3/(kilogram second2).

Light curve – a plot of how an object's brightness changes over time.

Light year – distance light travels in one year (9.461 trillion kilometers, over 63,000 A.U.). Used for interstellar distances.

Local noon – when the Sun is on an observer's meridian.

Long period comet – a comet with an orbit period of thousands to millions of years long that comes from the Oort cloud.

Longitude – used to specify position on the Earth, it is the number of degrees east or west of the 0° line going through Greenwich, England.

172

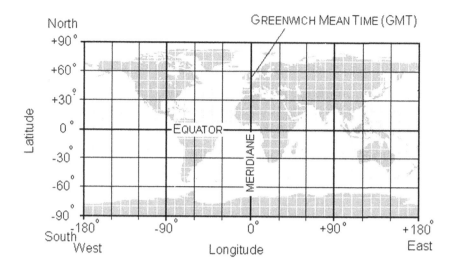

Mean Sun – imaginary object that moves uniformly eastward along the celestial equator such that it completes one 360° circuit of the sky in one year. The average solar day is the time between successive meridian crossings of the mean Sun.

Meridian – great circle on the sky that goes through the celestial poles and the zenith point. It separates the daytime motions of the Sun into ``a.m.'' and ``p.m.''. The azimuth of an object on the meridian in the northern sky = 0° and the azimuth of an object on the meridian in the southern sky = 180°.

Mesosphere – layer of a planet's atmosphere above a stratosphere where the temperature decreases with increasing altitude.

Meteor shower – what happens when the Earth passes through the dust trail left by a comet in its orbit? The dust grains are the size of a grain of sand or smaller and produce a large number of meteors in a short time that appear to come from a particular point in the sky.

Meteorite – a small rock from space that makes it to the surface of a planet without burning up in the planet's atmosphere. This distinguishes it from when it is passing through the atmosphere, glowing hot from the friction with the atmosphere and is called a meteor.

Microlens technique (planet detection) – a method of finding exoplanets by looking for the gravitational lensing effect from a planet orbiting a foreground star added to the gravitational lensing effect of the foreground star on the light from a more distant star.

Milky Way Galaxy – the large spiral galaxy in which our Sun and planets reside. Our Sun is one star of several hundred billion in the Milky Way.

Neap tide – tide that has a small change between low and high tide. It occurs at first and third quarter phase, when the Moon's tidal effect is perpendicular with the Sun's tidal effect.

Neutrino – a sub-atomic particle with very small mass that is produced in nuclear fusion reactions and rarely interacts with ordinary matter. Neutrinos travel at the nearly the speed of light and provide current information about the number of nuclear fusion reactions occurring in a star's core (in the case of the Sun, the information is only about 8.3 minutes old).

Neutron – subatomic particle with zero charge (neutral charge) that is found in the nucleus of an atom. It is slightly more massive than the positively-charged proton.

Neutron star – the collapsed core for an intermediate to high-mass star. The core is more than 1.4 solar masses but less than 3 solar masses and is about the diameter of a city. The pressure from degenerate neutrons prevents further collapse.

Newton – unit of force in the metric system. It is used to specify the amount of weight.

Newton's 1st law of motion – a body at rest remains at rest, and one moving in a straight line maintains a constant speed and same direction unless it is deflected by a force.

Newton's 2nd law of motion – the amount of force needed to cause an acceleration depends on an object's mass, such that the force applied = the mass of an object × its acceleration.

Newton's 3rd law of motion – for every action force ON an object, there is an equal but opposite force BY the object.

North celestial pole (NCP) – projection of the Earth's North Pole onto the sky. The NCP altitude = the observer's northern latitude.

Nova – an object that greatly increases in brightness rapidly, so it appears as a ``new star''. It is caused by the buildup on a white dwarf's surface of hydrogen gas from a companion star to the point where the hydrogen fuses explosively into helium. The super-rapid fusion does not blow up the white dwarf, so the process can repeat itself (contrast with a Type I supernova).

Nuclear fusion – the process used by stars to generate energy: less-massive nuclei are fused together under extremely high temperatures and densities to form more-massive nuclei plus some energy. The energy comes from the transformation of some of the mass into energy.

Nucleus (comet) – the ``dirty iceberg'' about the size of a city from which all of the stuff in a comet comes from. Irregularly-shaped it is made of dust and frozen gases.

Olbers' Paradox – the problem that if the universe is infinite in size and age, then the night sky should everywhere be as bright as the Sun because no matter which direction you look, your line of sight will see a star or galaxy.

Oort Cloud – a large spherical cloud of billions to trillions of comets surrounding the Sun at distances between roughly 50,000 to 100,000 A.U. from the Sun. It has not been directly observed; its presence is inferred from the behavior and orbits of the long period comets.

Open universe – a universe with too little matter (gravity) to stop the expansion (it has an ``open future'').

Ozone – a type of oxygen molecule made of three oxygen atoms bound together (O_3). This molecule absorbs ultraviolet light.

Parsec (pc) – distance at which an object would have a parallax of one arc second. Equals approximately 3.26 light years or about 206,265 astronomical units (A.U.).

Perihelion – point in an object's orbit around the Sun that is closest to the Sun.

Period-luminosity relation – how the average luminosity of Cepheid (variable star: a type of variable star that changes brightness by changing size and temperature with a period that depends on its average luminosity) variable stars depends on their period of pulsation.

Photon – a distinct ``chunk'' or particle of electromagnetic radiation.

Photon Photosphere – the thin layer of the Sun where the gas just becomes thin enough for the photons from the interior can escape to space. It is the ``surface'' of the Sun.

Photosynthesis – a process used by plants to convert water, carbon dioxide, and sunlight into carbohydrates and oxygen. The oxygen in the Earth's atmosphere is produced by this process.

Planetary nebula – final mass-loss stage for a dying low-mass star in which the outer layers are ejected during the core's collapse to form a white dwarf.

Plate tectonics – the scientific theory that describes the process of the movement of pieces of the Earth's crust (called "plates") and how it explains the Earth's surface geology.

Poor cluster – galaxy cluster with only a few tens of galaxies.

Population I (stars) – younger stars including the hot blue stars that have slightly elliptical orbits closely aligned with the disk plane of the Milky Way Galaxy. The youngest stars are found in the spiral arms of the galactic disk.

Population II (stars) – older, redder stars that have very elliptical orbits randomly oriented and are found in the stellar halo and bulge of the Milky Way Galaxy.

Precession – slow wobble of an object's rotation axis or an object's orbit. The precession of the Earth's rotation axis is caused by the gravitational pulls of the Sun and the Moon on the Earth's equatorial bulge.

Proton – positively-charged subatomic particle that is found in the nucleus of an atom. It has about 1800 times more mass than its negatively-charged electron counterpart.

Proton-proton chain – a nuclear fusion chain reaction used by most stars to generate energy. In a chain process involving three or more reactions, the net result is four hydrogen nuclei are fused together to form a helium nucleus plus energy.

Protostar – collapsing clump of dust and gas that will later become a star. The protostar is warm enough to produce a lot of infrared and some microwave radiation. Microwave energy is produced by the surrounding cocoon cloud.

Pulsar – young neutron star with a strong magnetic field and rapid rotation that produces beams of radiation out of its magnetic poles. If the beams cross our line of sight, we see the star ``pulsate'' (flash on and off).

Quasar – short for ``quasi-stellar radio source''. Quasars are the most luminous of active galaxies---they are the extremely active nuclei of otherwise normal galaxies. Quasars generate a huge amount of energy within very tiny volumes. Because they are most luminous things known, quasars can be seen at very large distances. Looking like blue stars, they can be distinguished from stars by the presence of broad emission lines instead of the narrow absorption lines of normal stars, their large redshifts because of their very large distances (see the Hubble Law), and many quasars are strong radio sources, unlike stars which have weak radio emission.

Radio galaxy – usually an elliptical galaxy emitting very large amounts of radio energy from the core (up to millions of times a typical galaxy's radio emission) and having strong radio emission from regions extending out several million light years from the galaxy nucleus.

Radioactive dating – a technique that gives absolute ages of a material (rather than merely relative ages) from the number of radioactive active atoms remaining in the material.

Reddening – the preferential scattering of the shorter wavelengths of light as it passes through a dust cloud, so that a large fraction of the bluer wavelengths of light are scattered away from your line of sight while a large fraction of the redder wavelengths of light make it through the dust cloud unaffected. Dust clouds in space make stars behind the dust clouds appear redder than they would be if the dust was not there.

Red giant – a dying star that has become large in diameter and cools on the surface while the core has shrunk and increased in temperature. Nuclear fusion takes place in a shell around the compressing core. They are more luminous than when the star was in the main sequence stage, even though their surface is cool, because they have a HUGE surface area. Therefore, they are plotted in the upper right part of the Hertzsprung Russel Diagram. The Hertzsprung– Russell diagram is a scatter graph of stars showing the relationship between the stars' absolute magnitudes or luminosity versus their spectral types or classifications and effective temperatures.

Redshift – the shift of spectral lines from an object to longer wavelengths because the object is moving away from the observer. The greater the speed of the object, the greater the redshift will be.

Reflector telescope – telescope that uses a large mirror at the back of the telescope to gather and focus the light. It has no size limit and is the type preferred for large research telescopes.

Refraction – the bending of waves when they pass from one transparent medium (or vacuum) to another (e.g., sunlight bending as it passes through the Earth's atmosphere).

Refractor telescope – telescope that uses a large glass lens at the front end of the telescope to gather and focus the light. The glass lens has a maximum size limit and suffers to some degree from chromatic aberration.

Rich cluster – a cluster of hundreds to thousands of galaxies.

Right ascension (RA) – position on the celestial sphere measured with respect to the vernal equinox position on the celestial equator. It is a projection of longitude lines onto the sky and converted to time units. An object's right ascension is fixed with respect to the stars. Varies from 0h at the vernal equinox point to 24h in a full circle.

Rotation curve – how the orbital velocities of objects in the disk of a spiral galaxy vary with increasing distance from the center of the galaxy. The rotation curve is used to study the distribution of mass in a galaxy.

RR Lyrae (variable star) – a type of low-mass variable stars that all have the same average luminosity. RR Lyrae are valuable for determining distances to star clusters.

Schwarzschild radius – the distance from a black hole's center at which the escape velocity equals the speed of light (same as the event horizon).

Seismology – the study of a planet's interior from observations of how seismic waves (``earthquake waves'') travel through the interior.

Seyfert galaxy – a spiral galaxy with a compact, very bright nucleus that produces a non-thermal continuous spectrum with broad (fat) emission lines on top.

Sidereal day – time between successive meridian crossings of a star. It is the true rotation period of a planet (on Earth, one sidereal day = 23 hours 56 minutes 4.09 seconds). Rotation rate of the Earth = 1° every 4 minutes (actually 3.989 minutes). The Earth's sidereal day is four minutes shorter than the solar day our clocks are based on so a star crosses the meridian 4 minutes earlier than it did the previous night.

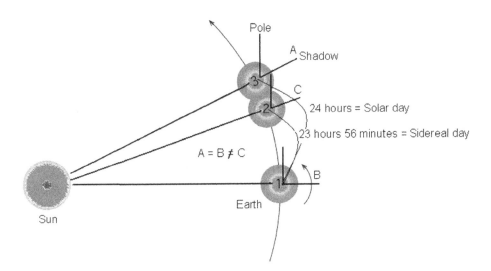

Sidereal period – the period of revolution of one object around another measured with respect to the stars (e.g., for the Moon, it is 27.3 days).

Sidereal year – the time required for the Earth to complete an exactly 360° orbit around the Sun as measured with respect to the stars = 365.2564 mean solar days (contrast with tropical year). A tropical year (also known as a solar year), for general purposes, is the length of time that the Sun takes to return to the same position in the cycle of seasons, as seen from Earth; for example, the time from vernal equinox to vernal equinox, or from summer solstice to summer solstice.

Solar day – time between successive meridian crossings of the Sun. Our clocks are based on this interval of time (on Earth, one solar day = 24 hours on average).

Solar eclipse – when the shadow of the Moon hits the Earth at exactly new phase. The Moon covers up part or all of the Sun.

Solar luminosity – unit of power relative to the Sun. One solar luminosity is about 4 x 1026 watts.

Solar mass – unit of mass relative to the Sun. One solar mass is about 2 x 1030 kilograms.

Solar neutrino problem – the number of neutrinos observed to be coming from the Sun's core is significantly less than what was predicted by the original solar interior models. Discovery of the oscillation of neutrino types solved the problem.

Solar wind – fast-moving, charged particles (mostly protons, electrons, and helium nuclei) flowing outward from the Sun's upper atmosphere, the corona.

Solstice – point on the sky where the ecliptic is furthest from the celestial equator by 23.5°. When the Sun is at the solstice point we have either the longest amount of daylight (summer: June 21 for northern hemisphere) or the shortest amount of daylight (winter: December 21 for northern hemisphere).

South celestial pole (SCP) – projection of the Earth's South Pole onto the sky. The SCP altitude = the observer's southern latitude.

Spacetime – the four-dimensional combination of space (three dimensions) and time (the fourth dimension). As a consequence of Special Relativity, time and space are not independent of each other and are relative to the motion of an observer.

Special Relativity – a theory invented by Albert Einstein to describe measurements of length and time for objects moving at constant velocity. Although it applies to all motion at constant velocity, it must be used instead of Newton's laws of motion at speeds of greater than about ten percent the speed of light.

Speckle interferometry – method that compensates for atmospheric turbulence by taking many fast exposures of an object to freeze the effect of seeing. Computer processing of the multiple exposures removes atmospheric and instrument distortions to produce high-resolution images at the telescope's theoretical resolving power.

Spectral type (also spectral class) – the classification of a star according to its temperature as measured from the strengths of its spectral lines. In order of temperatures from hottest to coolest the spectral types are O B A F G K M. This is also the order of luminosity and mass (most luminous and most massive to dimmest and least massive).

Spectroscopic binary – two stars orbiting a common point at too great a distance away from us to resolve the two stars individually, but whose binary nature is indicated in the periodic shift of their spectral lines as they orbit around each other.

Spectroscopic parallax – a method of determining distances to stars from knowledge of the luminosity of their spectral types and measurement of their apparent brightness. The distances are derived from the inverse square law of light brightness.

Spectroscopy – the analysis of an object from its spectrum.

Spectrum – display of the intensity of light at different wavelengths or frequencies.

Spherical aberration – a defect seen in images that is caused by the objective not being exactly shaped (e.g., an objective mirror not being exactly parabolic) so that not all of the light is focused to the same point.

Spiral galaxy – a highly flattened galaxy with a disk and a central bulge. The disk has a spiral pattern with slightly more stars and gas than in the rest of the disk. A slow, steady star formation rate means that they still have gas and dust left in them from which stars are still forming. The star orbits are constrained to stay within a small distance from the mid-plane of the disk and have small eccentricities.

Starburst galaxy – a galaxy undergoing a large burst of star formation usually as a result of a collision or merger of two galaxies. It can produce as much light as several hundred ``normal'' undisturbed galaxies.

Stefan-Boltzmann law – relation between the amount of energy emitted by a unit area on an object producing a thermal spectrum and its temperature: energy in Joules emitted by one square meter = $5.67 \times 10-8 \times$ temperature4. The temperature is in Kelvin.

Stellar nucleosynthesis – the creation of more massive nuclei from the fusion of less-massive nuclei inside stars. Just about all of the elements heavier than helium on the Earth were originally created via stellar nucleosynthesis.

Stratosphere – layer of a planet's atmosphere above a troposphere where temperature rises with increasing altitude because of the absorption of ultraviolet light.

Sublime – the turning of a solid directly into a gas without going through the intermediate liquid phase, e.g. the vapor of ``dry ice'' (the sublimation of frozen carbon dioxide).

Sunspot – cooler region on the Sun's surface that is a region of intense magnetic fields and is associated with solar activity. Because a sunspot is 1000 to 1500 K cooler, it is dimmer than the surrounding surface. The number of sunspots is greater when the Sun is more active.

Supercluster – a grouping of galaxy clusters pulled together by their mutual gravitational attraction to produce long, thin structures up to a few hundred megaparsecs long with large voids devoid of galaxies between the superclusters.

Supergiant – a dying star of extremely high luminosity and relatively cool surface temperature. Their diameters are over 100 times that of the Sun.

Supernova – for Type II supernova: final huge mass-loss stage for a dying high-mass star where the outer layers are ejected during the core's collapse to form a neutron star. A Type I supernova is the result of enough hydrogen accreted onto a white dwarf's surface to put the white dwarf beyond the Chandresekhar limit. The white dwarf collapses and the super-rapid fusion blows the white dwarf apart (contrast with a nova). The luminosity of a supernova can temporarily be as much as an entire galaxy of billions of stars.

Synodic period – the time required for a planet or moon to go from a particular configuration with respect to the Sun back to that same configuration (e.g., for the Moon, it is the time to go from a given phase back to the same phase--- 29.5 days).

Telescope – device used to gather and focus electromagnetic radiation. A telescope extends the power of human vision by making objects brighter, sharper, and larger, as well as, imaging objects in wavelengths that are not detectable by the human eye.

Time zone – interval of longitudes 15 degrees wide in which every clock is set to the same time (e.g., every clock in the Pacific Time zone will give the same time).

Total solar eclipse – a type of solar eclipse that happens when the Sun and Moon are exactly lined up and the Moon is close enough to the Earth to totally block the Sun's surface (see the annular eclipse).

Tropical year – the time interval between two successive vernal equinoxes = 365.2422 mean solar days (contrast with sidereal year).

Ttroposphere – lowest layer of a planet's atmosphere (closest to the surface) where the temperature decreases with increasing altitude and where convection is important. Clouds form in here. Greenhouse effect is present.

T-Tauri (star) – young star that is just beginning nuclear fusion and produces strong outflows of particles (winds) that clears away the gas and dust from which the star formed.

21-cm line radiation – emission line in the radio band by cool, neutral atomic hydrogen that is used to map the structure of the Milky Way and other galaxies because it passes easily through dust in the interstellar medium.

Vernal equinox – specific moment in the year (on March 21) when the Sun is directly on the celestial equator, moving north of the celestial equator.

Wavelength – the distance between two crests or two troughs of a wave.

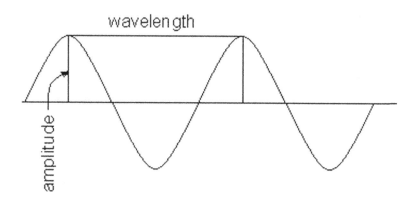

White dwarf – The core is less than 1.4 solar masses and is about the diameter of the Earth. The pressure from degenerated electrons prevents further collapse.

Wien's law – relation between the wavelength of maximum emission in a thermal spectrum and its temperature: wavelength peak in nanometers = 2.9× 106/temperature in Kelvin.

Zenith – point on the celestial sphere that is always directly above the observer regardless of his/her location.

Zodiac – narrow belt of twelve constellation centered on the ecliptic.